Empowered Families,
Thriving Students

Dedications:

W. B. Collado:

To my family, your unconditional love and pride in my work as an educator are my sources of strength and inspiration. My sincere gratitude goes to my mother, my aunts, and my uncles, who dedicated their lives to teaching with over 150 years of collective service and were great educators: Maria (my mother), Tia Dominica, Tia Juanita, Tia Ana, Tia Simona, and Padrino Victor. It is an honor to follow in your footsteps.

Alex Marrero:

Bendición, ma. *This book is dedicated to you, Mirtha—my first teacher and greatest example of sacrificial love.* Me enseñaste que la educación empieza en la casa, *and you lived that truth with quiet strength and relentless faith. You bore every hardship so Manolin and I could have every opportunity. Your resilience and unconditional love are the foundation of this work.*

To my wife, Suzy—thank you for your unwavering support. Your grace, strength, and patience make it possible for me to pursue this mission with purpose.

To my children, Alexa and Axel—you are the reason I strive to build a more empowered future for all families. Your laughter, questions, and wonder keep me grounded and dreaming.

This book is born of sacrifice, sustained by love, and dedicated to the enduring power of family.

Belinda Reyes:

To my husband, Alex, and our children—Vidal, Gabriel, and Sofia—thank you for being my source of pride, joy, and inspiration. Your love reminds me daily of the purpose behind this work.

To every parent who shows up, speaks up, and lifts up their children, you are the heart of this book. And to the educators who partner with families and open doors for shared success, your dedication leads the way.

Above all, and second only to God, I honor my mother, Virginia Hernandez. Her unwavering faith in me and her example of true community service, recognized as the School District of Osceola County Senior Volunteer of the Year, have shaped my deepest understanding of family engagement. Her love is a legacy and the spirit of Ubuntu: I Am Because We Are.

What Your Colleagues Are Saying . . .

"Drs. Collado, Marrero, and Reyes have provided the 'why' and the 'how to' of empowering families to create thriving students from a personal perspective! It is filled with keen, practical and useful strategies to help administrators and teachers make the connections that are critical for students' success."

Mary Ellen Elia
Commissioner of Education, New York
President, Success for Students, Inc.
Tampa, Florida

"*Empowered Families, Thriving Students* provides clear strategies and wonderful wisdom. This is a must read for anyone committed to helping children flourish in school and in life."

Ulysses Navarrete
Executive Director, Association of Latino
Administrators and Superintendents
Washington, DC

"Drs. Collado, Marrero, and Reyes turn belief into behavior, translating respect for community wisdom into daily practice and treating trust as disciplined work. By recognizing families as partners, the authors give leaders practical steps to improve relationships and student learning."

Nancy B. Gutiérrez
President & Lead Executive Officer,
The Leadership Academy
New York, New York

"This book is a very practical approach to engaging families as authentic partners in the education of their children. The authors present a strong case for student success that is grounded in a systematic plan of action that engages all the collaborators who shape students' experiences and learning environments."

John Hardman
Senior Instructor, IDEAL Program Director, Department of
Educational Leadership and Research Methodology,
College of Education, Florida Atlantic University
Boca Raton, Florida

"*Empowered Families, Thriving Students* is a clear, actionable roadmap for schools ready to stop talking about family engagement and start building it. One of the most powerful examples illustrated how a school reimagined the role of the family liaison—connecting families through cultural events, personal outreach, and leadership opportunities. This is what real partnership looks like."

Brad Johnson
#3 Global Guru in Education
Author, *Room 212* and *Coffee with the Custodian*
Cumming, Georgia

"A powerful tool for educators, for not only planning on how to enhance parents' participation, but also for self-reflection. It is critical that we educators stop perpetuating deficit-based mindsets. This book offers vignettes, action steps, and most importantly addresses anti-bias and culturally relevant competencies."

Maria C. Castilleja
Retired Executive Director of Curriculum and Instruction
Sweetwater Union High School District
Long Beach, California

"*Empowered Families, Thriving Students* empowers educators to lead with heart, serve with purpose, and rise to their highest calling."

Consuelo Castillo Kickbusch
Founder and CEO, Educational Achievement Services, Inc.
Henderson, Nevada

"*Empowered Families, Thriving Students* is an inspiring and practical guide that shows how strong school-family partnerships can transform education. The authors offer clear strategies, real-world examples, and a hopeful vision for building trust and collaboration between educators and caregivers."

Gustavo Balders
Superintendent, Beaverton School District
AASA, President
ALAS, Past President
Beaverton, Oregon

Empowered Families, Thriving Students

Unlocking the Potential of Family–School Partnerships

Washington B. Collado

Alex Marrero

Belinda Reyes

Foreword by Douglas B. Reeves

CORWIN

FOR INFORMATION:

Corwin

A Sage Company

2455 Teller Road

Thousand Oaks, California 91320

(800) 233-9936

www.corwin.com

Sage Publications Ltd.

1 Oliver's Yard

55 City Road

London EC1Y 1SP

United Kingdom

Sage Publications India Pvt. Ltd.

10th Floor, Emaar Capital Tower 2

MG Road, Sikanderpur

Sector 26, Gurugram

Haryana - 122002

India

Sage Publications Asia-Pacific Pte. Ltd.

18 Cross Street #10-10/~1/12

China Square Central

Singapore 048423

Vice President and Editorial
  Director: Monica Eckman

Senior Acquisitions Editor: Pam Berkman

Content Development
  Manager: Desirée A. Bartlett

Senior Editorial Assistant: Nyle De Leon

Production Editor: Tori Mirsadjadi

Copy Editor: Denise McIntyre

Typesetter: C&M Digitals (P) Ltd.

Proofreader: Jennifer Grubba

Cover Designer: Candice Harman

Printed and bound by CPI Group (UK) Ltd, Croydon, CR0 4YY

Paperback ISBN 978-1-0719-7888-7

Library of Congress Control Number: 2025947830

This book is printed on acid-free paper.

25 26 27 28 29 10 9 8 7 6 5 4 3 2 1

CONTENTS

CHAPTER 2. OVERCOMING DEFICIT-BASED VIEWS 31

CHAPTER 3. ESTABLISHING TRUST FOR LASTING RELATIONSHIPS 47

CHAPTER 6. STRENGTHENING STUDENTS' ACADEMIC POTENTIAL: EMPOWERING FAMILIES WITH PRACTICAL WAYS TO PROVIDE SUPPORT   105

FOREWORD

BY DOUGLAS B. REEVES[1]

In this immensely practical book, Washington Collado, Alex Marrero, and Belinda Reyes have provided an exceptional guide for school leaders, teachers, families, and community leaders for collaborating to support student success by fostering family empowerment. Although many books are long on philosophy and short on practical application, this book is precisely the opposite. Whatever your role in the educational system or community, you will find practical guidance on the what, why, and how of supporting the kind of family empowerment that leads to student success.

---

[1]Dr. Reeves is the author of more than 40 books and 100 articles on educational leadership. Twice named to the Harvard University Distinguished Authors Series, Doug is the recipient of several national and international awards for his contributions to education. He has shared his research in 50 states and more than 40 countries. He can be reached at Douglas.Reeves@ CreativeLeadership.net or 781 710 9633.

The 14 strategies included in the following pages provide essential guides for school and community leaders on how to forge the essential collaboration among families, teachers, students, community leaders, and educational leaders to focus on student achievement and well-being. What is especially impressive about this book is the relentless focus on student success. Although the authors recognize the challenges that new arrivals to the United States face, they make no excuses but rather challenge all of us, from first-generation to eighth-generation residents, to support our neighbors and ourselves in building stronger communities. It is especially impressive that the authors challenge us to go beyond traditional "meetings and meals" to get to substantive communication among all community members.

An especially important element of this book is the use of a combination of nationally recognized evidence and the personal experience of the authors. It is too often the case that even the best-intentioned advocacy for students slides into polemics. This book prefers evidence and rejects rhetoric. The end goal is not justification based on the oppression of underserved students, but rather the success of these students despite the challenges that they have faced. In sum, the strategies are practical, the vignettes are authentic, and the evidence is compelling. This is a book not merely to be read, but to be studied and discussed in community-wide forums.

—Douglas Reeves
Boston, Massachusetts

ACKNOWLEDGMENTS

We sincerely thank the educators who dedicate their lives to engaging and empowering families, building communities rooted in love, trust, and shared purpose—places where students can truly thrive. To the families who generously contribute their time, whether through involvement, participation, or advocacy, your selfless commitment serves as a meaningful reminder and a source of inspiration. Together, your efforts strengthen the gratitude that families and communities feel for educators because they see teaching as a calling made stronger through partnership. Our students deserve every moment of collaboration. A heartfelt thank-you to all the educators and families whose voices and stories inspired the vignettes in this book. You brought heart, truth, and hope to these pages, and we are deeply grateful. May this book serve as a guiding light for collaboration, understanding, and the endless possibilities that come when schools and families work as one.

Publisher's Acknowledgments

Corwin gratefully acknowledges the contributions of the following reviewers:

Helene Alalouf
Instructional Coach
and Adjunct Education Professor, Touro University
New York, New York

Beverly B. Allen-Hardy
Assistant Professor, University of Richmond
Retired K–12 Public School Administrator,
Henrico County Public Schools
Richmond, Virgina

Chris Hubbuch
Assistant Superintendent, Fulton Public Schools
Fulton, Missouri

Joann Hulquist
Adjunct Professor, George Fox University
West Linn, Oregon

Louis Lim
Principal, Bur Oak Secondary School
Markham, Ontario, Canada

Tanna Nicely
Elementary Principal, South Knoxville Elementary
Adjunct Professor, Carson Newman University
Blaine, Tennessee

Melissa Nixon
Senior Executive Director, Federal and Special Programs,
Guilford County Schools
High Point, North Carolina

Catherine Sosnowski
Adjunct Professor, Central Connecticut State University
Bristol, Connecticut

Candace B. Wilkerson
Director of Elementary Education,
Henrico County Public Schools
Crozier, Virgina

ABOUT THE AUTHORS

Dr. Washington "Nino" B. Collado was born in the Dominican Republic, in a small town called Jánico (Ha-Nee-Co). His mother, María Tejada, along with seven of his uncles and aunts, were all teachers. After his mother's death, Dr. Collado and his three sisters moved to the United States to live with their father in New York City.

After earning his bachelor's degree from Queens College, Dr. Collado taught Spanish and English as a Second Language in New York City Public Schools. He and his family then moved to Florida where he taught in Miami-Dade Public Schools. He later joined Broward County Public Schools' Multicultural Department to develop curricula and provide training for teachers and administrators on the contributions of Latinos, African Americans, and women throughout U.S. history. He became an assistant principal at Broward County Public Schools and later served as a principal. He has spent 17 years as a principal at the middle and high school levels and served as president of the Broward Principals and Assistants Association (BPAA). During this time, he earned his doctorate in Educational Leadership from Florida Atlantic University.

In February 2021, Dr. Nino Collado received the Principal of the Year award for Broward County Public Schools, the sixth-largest school district in the country. Dr. Collado is currently an adjunct professor at Florida Atlantic University, where he teaches courses on educational leadership and serves as an associate at Creative Leadership Solutions.

Throughout his career, Dr. Nino Collado has dedicated a significant portion of his time to teaching and mentoring others. He has traveled to numerous countries and more than 30 states as a motivational speaker on topics related to school leadership and family engagement. He has also appeared as a panelist on CNN Español, NPR (New York), Telemundo, Univision, and others. Additionally, he has written more than 100 articles for newspapers and magazines, including the *Miami Herald*, and has authored or coauthored six books, including his latest book *Four Pillars to Guide Visionary Educators* (2025). He and his wife Carmen R. Collado are proud parents of four sons: Mario, Alejandro, Miguel, and Victor.

Dr. Alex Marrero has served as the Superintendent of Denver Public Schools since the Spring of 2021. As the son of a Cuban refugee and a Dominican immigrant, Dr. Marrero understands the diverse needs of his students firsthand and advocates for them. Under his leadership, Denver Public Schools has achieved its highest-ever graduation rates, increased proficiency rates to all-time highs, and implemented its first-ever equity-based strategic plan. His efforts have significantly raised salaries and established living wages for all employees, while enhancing school safety and cybersecurity. His strategies have successfully moved over two dozen schools off the State Accountability Clock. Dr. Marrero established the Latine Education Advisory Council (LEAC) to enhance educational outcomes for Latino/Hispanic students, launched the International Educators Institute to aid new international teachers in adapting to the educational system and community, and opened Community Hubs throughout the city and county of Denver. These hubs connect students, families, and community members with free services to increase their economic self-sufficiency and academic success.

Dr. Marrero's leadership has been widely recognized with several awards, including Superintendent of the Year by the District Administration Leadership Institute and the Colorado Association of Latino/a Administrators and Superintendents, for 2024. District Administration named him one of the Top 100 Influencers in Education in 2024. He was named a "Superintendent to Watch" in 2022 by the National School Public Relations Association (NSPRA) and one of "5 Superintendents to Watch in 2023" by the organization K–12 Dive.

Beyond his role in Denver, Dr. Marrero is deeply involved in educational leadership on a national scale. He serves as president of the Association of Latino Administrators and Superintendents and an Executive Board Member for the Council of Great City Schools where he also is the Chair of the taskforce for Boys of Color. The U.S. Secretary of Homeland Security invited him to serve on the Homeland Security Academic Partnership Council and Colorado's governor also selected him to serve on the Business Experiential Learning (BEL) Commission. In addition to these various roles, he holds adjunct professorships at Boston University, Manhattan University, and St. Peters University.

Dr. Marrero's leadership philosophy is centered on empowering every student, regardless of their background, to overcome obstacles and become innovative leaders in their fields, reflecting his personal journey and commitment to educational excellence.

Dr. Belinda Reyes is the Chief Executive Officer of Reyes Executive Coaching and Leadership Solutions and serves as an adjunct instructor at the University of Central Florida. In the K–12 school system, she has served as media clerk, teacher, and in various district and school capacities including principal, and most recently assistant superintendent. Dr. Reyes has dedicated herself to advancing education at all levels. She has earned accolades as a turnaround leader and mentor, making significant strides in addressing achievement gaps among Hispanic students and narrowing disparities between Black students and their peers. As a researcher–practitioner, her contributions to dual-language education have been widely recognized, with her research published in peer-reviewed journals such as the *Florida Sunshine State TESOL Journal* and the *University of Central Florida Journal of English Learner Education*. Her work has reached audiences in 47 countries, reflecting her global influence.

A staunch advocate for public education's role in strengthening democracy, Dr. Reyes has presented at prestigious forums, including the International Associate of Scholastic Excellence (INTASE) World EduLead conference in the Asia Pacific region, where her expertise in global citizenship and educational innovation was showcased. Dr. Reyes' efforts focus on fostering systems that engage families, enhance instruction, and accelerate learning for vulnerable populations, ensuring equitable access to quality education for all. Dr. Reyes was awarded the 2025 American College of Education Alumni Achievement Award in recognition of her exceptional leadership and outstanding service.

Beyond her professional roles, Dr. Reyes is dedicated to mentoring future educational leaders. She has guided emerging administrators within her district and beyond, including through organizations such as Florida Association of Latino Administrators and Superintendents (ALAS). As a graduate of the national ALAS Superintendent Leadership Academy and the American Association of School Administrators Aspiring Superintendents Academy for Women Leaders, Dr. Reyes is committed to developing skilled leaders who empower diverse communities.

INTRODUCTION

In our extensive experiences as principals, teachers, superintendents, and as parents ourselves, we can assert that
most educators and families agree that family and community engagement strengthen our schools, their operational
practices, and academic outcomes. The collaborative efforts of
families and educators create a powerful force for supporting
students academically and socioemotionally. Often, the aspi-
ration to create a structure for effective family and community
engagement in school systems is reduced to a well-elaborated
vision statement without any framework for its implementation in daily practice and planning. However, it does not have
to be that way. Instead, we offer an evidence-based process to
cultivate the family partnership with school that we, as educators, aspire to have at our schools.

Our purpose in writing this book has been practical and aspi-
rational: to provide educators, school leaders, and community
advocates with an actionable framework for building strong,

equitable, and culturally responsive relationships with families that ultimately drive student success. Family engagement is not a side initiative nor a one-time event; it is the foundation of sustainable educational progress. However, in too many school systems, it remains undervalued or poorly executed. This book aims to change that by offering a cohesive roadmap that moves from foundational trust to transformational partnership.

Laying the Foundation: Vision, Equity, and Trust

Chapter 1, From Vision to Action: Crafting Tailored Family Engagement Plans, opens with a clear call to engage with purpose. It then introduces readers to the necessity of designing school– or district-specific family engagement plans.

Too often, families from minoritized backgrounds, whether due to race, socioeconomic status (SES), language, or immigration status, are perceived through a deficit lens. Chapter 2, Overcoming Deficit-Based Views, guides educators in recognizing and dismantling these views, replacing them with asset-based strategies that activate families as coeducators, celebrate cultural storytelling, and emphasize the role of empowerment.

Trust becomes the connective tissue in Chapter 3, Establishing Trust for Lasting Relationships. Without trust, even the most well-designed engagement plan will falter. Through community scans, asset-based celebrations, and a focus on physical and psychological safety, this chapter examines how schools can become places where families feel seen, heard, and valued.

Chapter 4, Building Capacity for Authentic Partnership, introduces a three-tier model of involvement, engagement, and empowerment, helping educators assess their school's current state and its potential for growth. We offer readers guidance on crafting context-specific family engagement frameworks that evolve as families take on deeper roles within the school community. We highlight the Family Leadership Institute as a powerful vision of what can happen when families are given the tools to lead, advocate, and inspire systemic change, moving from partnership to leadership.

Expanding the scope of engagement beyond the school walls, Chapter 5, Building Lasting Community Partnerships, emphasizes the power of the village. It showcases how local organizations, institutions, and businesses can become allies in student achievement. Educators are guided through strategies to build, sustain, and celebrate community partnerships that reflect and reinforce the cultural pride and social capital of the neighborhoods they serve. This chapter affirms that schools cannot and should not do this work alone.

Chapter 6, Strengthening Students' Academic Potential, addresses one of the most critical goals of engagement: supporting academic success. Whether families are navigating early literacy milestones or preparing their children for postsecondary pathways, this chapter provides frameworks and strategies for building families' academic knowledge and efficacy. These strategies encourage schools to align goals, provide accessible training, and foster two-way feedback loops that position families as academic partners.

Chapter 7, Reimagining Traditional Practices for Greater Family Empowerment—the final chapter—reimagines traditional events such as Open House and parent–teacher conferences as opportunities for transformative relationship building. This chapter encourages educators to embrace innovative approaches that foster leadership, agency, and shared purpose.

Features and Benefits

This book is intended as a practical tool full of implementable strategies. To that end, each chapter has features that are designed to enable you to adapt the strategies to your specific context so that you can implement them in culturally responsive ways. Our goal is not only to explain the "why" but also to facilitate the "how."

- Each chapter is focused on two strategies aimed at empowering families.

- The strategies are illustrated by vignettes. These are stories drawn from the authors' personal experiences with schools and families. Although fictionalized for the purposes of illustration, each story is based on actual events.

- Each strategy concludes with clear and implementable action steps so that you can immediately put this text to good use.

- Because empowering families requires that we analyze our own mindsets and preconceptions, each strategy is followed by self-analysis questions to prompt your thinking and reflection.

- Each chapter ends with Chapter Takeaways highlighting the key points of the chapter.

- Each chapter ends with Reflection Questions for large, big-picture questions on the theme of the chapter.

A Call to Reflective Action

This book serves as a guide for those seeking concrete, research-informed strategies to strengthen family–school partnerships. It is a mirror that asks educators to reflect on their own beliefs, biases, and practices. Moreover, it serves as a manifesto for a more equitable and inclusive education system—one where families are not merely guests but cocreators of the learning experience. Let us begin this work together, not as a checklist to complete, but as a commitment to uphold.

The 14 strategies presented throughout this journey are not abstract ideals; they are grounded, research informed, and tested in various educational settings. Each strategy is connected to practical examples, reflective questions, and action steps that encourage readers to pause, plan, and personalize the approach within their schools and communities.

This book is a guide and a call to action. It argues that when families are genuinely engaged and involved as partners, leaders, and cultural assets, the outcome is not only stronger schools but also more just and vibrant communities. We welcome you to join us on the journey to authentically cultivating the power of family and community engagement in our schools.

FROM VISION TO ACTION: CRAFTING TAILORED FAMILY ENGAGEMENT PLANS

> "Historically, the family has played the primary role in educating children for life, with the school providing supplemental scaffolding to the family." ●
>
> —Stephen Covey (1989)

All families bring a colorful tapestry of various cultures and histories to the school community. When these histories and cultures are shared with the school and other families, the school becomes a vibrant community that celebrates and honors family backgrounds as welcome assets to the school. We encourage educators to embrace the challenge of learning about their students' home lives and identifying the strengths that families offer, so that they, in turn, can develop engagement plans that incorporate those traditions and strengths. This chapter delves deeper into encouraging educators to take responsibility and ownership for developing cultural competency, specifically tailored to their unique context and community. Strategies 1 and 2 provide examples and action plans to enable you to foster family leadership and advocacy in culturally relevant ways.

Taking on the responsibility to center engagement efforts on the needs of the people we serve requires learning about the obstacles and taking actions to remove them. In our experience, families are more likely to attend fun after-school events that welcome their entire family. To encourage participation in other, perhaps less fun, school activities, we have found that it is essential to make them feel welcome, to consider creative options for the care of younger siblings to free up families' attention, and to act with the mindset that families want to be involved and want to put in the effort. After taking inventory of the current level of family engagement, the next step is to strategically plan to strengthen family voice and active family leadership. Chapter 1 presents two strategies to facilitate the creation of a strategic plan that transitions from family engagement to family empowerment.

STRATEGY 1

Develop a School- or District-Specific Engagement Plan ●

STRATEGY 2

Establish Collaborative Goal Setting and Family Participation in Decision Making ●

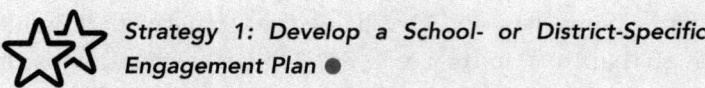

Strategy 1: Develop a School- or District-Specific Engagement Plan ●

Developing a school- or district-specific engagement plan ensures that the unique needs of your school and community are met. Identifying action plans that value the individual contributions of the families in your community, as well as the contributions of your school to this partnership, deepens the partnership. Schools can collaborate with families and community members to create engagement plans tailored to their school community's unique characteristics. This involves assessing community needs, cultural values, and available resources to design initiatives that resonate with families. Work must occur to build understanding and foster mutual respect, creating meaningful and actionable plans for engagement. The following vignette illustrates how Principal Reyes successfully created context-specific engagement plans informed by efforts to learn about the specific needs of the families in her school community.

 **Addressing the Disconnect Between Perception and Reality**

Lancaster Elementary in Orlando, Florida, was built in the 1960s to accommodate the needs of military families. When the military base closed, the community experienced a shift in population—people of color became the majority group in the community. Lancaster Elementary began serving as a One-Way Developmental Center for multilingual learners and housing units for students with disabilities. A significant amount of the population was unhoused or indefinitely displaced while living in rundown pay-by-the-week hotels, with 98% of the students qualifying for free or reduced lunch. In 2006, Principal Belinda Reyes was appointed to lead the school and worked diligently to change mindsets: to educate the educated and to learn from those who had not had access to a formal education.

Change staff mindsets, change practices

School faculty and staff took ownership of their responsibility for identifying and addressing the disconnect between the staff's perception and the reality of the families. The staff at the school were extremely committed to the success of the students, but they held expectations for families based on their own middle-class experiences. Changing educators' mindsets when working with immigrant and impoverished families requires empathy, education, and a commitment to fostering strong, inclusive relationships. Principal Reyes recognized that the most effective way to change mindsets was to modify practices and enable faculty, staff, and families to have positive interactions with one another. Staff perception evolved to the point

(Continued)

(Continued)

where staff could recognize the barriers preventing some families from fully participating. Additionally, staff learned to create an environment of support that allowed families to be fully engaged in their children's education.

Learning how class differences affect behavior and mindsets

The first step was engaging the teachers and leadership team in Ruby K. Payne's "A Framework for Understanding Poverty" workshop (based on Payne, 2005). In this workshop, they gained skills in several topics, including using strategies to impact the achievement of students living below the poverty line, understanding how economic class affects behaviors and mindset, and developing stronger relationships. As they reflected on potential biases and assumptions, Principal Reyes began making home visits with teachers to foster relationships in a safe environment for families.

Make context-specific changes based on your findings

Using what they learned from the workshop and the home visits, the staff began to make changes in how they designed family engagement goals and practices. On an annual basis, the principal, teacher, families, and students created a school engagement plan tailored to each family. Upon completion, the plan was a written understanding and commitment to the roles each plays in the student's academic and social-emotional well-being. Although the school had a position of Family Liaison to provide basic resources and school supplies, Principal Reyes reimagined the position to intentionally connect families in all areas of the school in addition to providing basic needs and connections to social services.

Mrs. Caterina Morelli, the Family Liaison, was essential in ensuring each plan was executed with fidelity. As an Italian American, Mrs. Morelli did not share the same cultural background as the multilingual learners at her schools; therefore, she made it her business to learn about the students' cultures and get to know the families on a personal level. The respect she showed to families earned Mrs. Morelli the trust and respect she needed to connect with them on a deeper level. Families became excited about contributing to the school. After learning about the talents individual families could offer, Mrs. Morelli provided opportunities for them to contribute by creating volunteering opportunities tailored to those talents. Some of their personal favorites were creating a school friendship garden and stocking the school store. These were activities families could do during the school day while caring for their young children.

Mrs. Morelli also addressed other barriers. She ensured that the meetings for the Parent–Teacher Organization and School Advisory Committee occurred one after the other during a time that families had identified as ideal for increasing family participation. Staff maximized the presence of a captive audience by using that time to celebrate student progress toward school goals and to share with families the impact they were making in their children's education.

Continue learning

Family surveys were used to further engage families. Survey data led to the creation of honor roll assemblies every quarter—this event was a favorite among families. Although common in many schools, this was the first time families at Lancaster Elementary had the opportunity to celebrate their children's accomplishments in this public forum. Instituting honor roll assemblies was a way to communicate positively about students' academic and behavioral achievements and the high expectations that the school, staff, and families had for all students. The result was that an increasing number of children met these high expectations.

Students seeing their families involved in school, coupled with increased communication, led to an increase in academic achievement and a decrease in behavior referrals, allowing teachers and students to maximize instructional time. The sense of pride shared by students, families, and teachers alike was unmatched. ●

The critical work of family engagement happens at the school level, where relationships are built through daily interactions. Whether it is at the bus stop, family pick-up line, or school event, relationships are initiated in those micromoments. School districts can also support district-wide outreach efforts by providing schools with training and support to conduct these outreach efforts. The following vignette provides an example of such work in action.

 ## Designing Engagement to Meet the Specific Needs of Specific Families

Hurricane Maria was a catastrophic hurricane that caused over 2,200 K–12 students to seek shelter in Osceola County, Florida, in November 2017. The superintendent gathered district leaders to clearly convey the message that these students were not "displaced students," they are *our students*, and the district and community would work together to ensure their acclimation and success during this time of transition.

The Multicultural Education Department was composed of highly skilled, dedicated, and caring individuals with a passion and purpose for serving students. Mrs. Naira Alvira served as the Bilingual Community Liaison and reached out to other departments and community organizations for support. Multiple regional "family gatherings" were scheduled at the high schools where traditional Puerto Rican food (such as arroz con gandules, pernil, y flan) was served. At the same time, students and staff played salsa music as well as "La Borinqueña," known as the Puerto Rican national anthem, to welcome and honor the heritage of the new families. All displaced families and their hosts in Florida were invited to participate in the experience, which included booths offering various community resources, free uniforms and clothing, meal vouchers, free haircuts, and classes for families.

Although all the resources were valuable, the family classes were vital. These classes provided families with the opportunity to learn about their rights and responsibilities regarding their children's education. For example, they were provided with the name and contact information of the specific school-based English for Speakers of Other Languages (ESOL) Education Specialist, who would provide translation services, serve as an advocate for their child, and act as a liaison between the family and the school. Understanding the attendance policy was also key. Many came from Puerto Rico, where many schools did not have substitute teachers. This meant that when the teacher was absent, there was no school. In contrast, the United States has a policy of mandatory attendance for students, and schools provide substitute teachers to ensure that education is not disrupted.

To emphasize that the school intended to meet the context-specific needs of the families in this community, the family gatherings were conducted in

Spanish. After a warm welcome, families had the opportunity to choose which booths to visit and which classes to attend. Topics included the importance of attendance, academic support, ESOL accommodations for learning, who to ask for what, and the hidden norms of the school system. Families were invited to engage in dialogue, not only with district staff but also with one another. They laughed and cried together. Together, they brought the room to life. ●

The following suggested actions are offered as a guide for creating a context-specific engagement plan in your school or district.

ACTION STEPS

 For Developing a Context-Specific Engagement Plan

- Provide faculty and staff with cultural competency training that highlights diverse cultural backgrounds, experiences, and challenges to foster mutual respect.

- Provide faculty and staff with resources, support, and cultural competency training that highlights the particular needs of students living below the poverty line.

- Promote relationship building through home visits and open communication where families can share their perspectives.

- Challenge faculty and staff to engage in self-reflection and set an expectation of asset-based thinking.

- Provide support systems for families by connecting them to social services, English language classes, and needed school supplies.

- Celebrate diversity through cultural events and curricular materials that reflect the cultural history and practice of your context-specific student population.

- Commit to building trust over time and showing genuine care. This is vital to authentically engaging families. ●

ACTIVITY

Develop a Context-Specific Engagement Plan for Your School

Please consider the steps and actions offered in the Action Plan below. Take a moment to reflect on how these steps can be applied to your school community. Use the column on the right to jot down your ideas on how you might tailor these steps in your school or district.

CONDUCT CULTURAL COMPETENCY TRAINING		
Step	Actions	Identify next steps to support these actions in the context of your school or system
Partner with organizations or experts specializing in cultural awareness and equity in education to deliver professional learning workshops.	• Include interactive activities, such as role-playing and case studies, to help faculty and staff understand diverse cultural backgrounds and experiences. • Schedule regular follow-ups and reflection sessions to reinforce learning and address new challenges.	

PROMOTE RELATIONSHIP BUILDING		
Step	Actions	Identify next steps to support these actions in the context of your school or system
Organize Home Visits	• Make home visits a team effort, ensuring educators are paired with translators if needed, to connect meaningfully with families in their own spaces.	
Implement Open Communication Systems	• Implement open communication systems such as multilingual newsletters, family forums, and real-time messaging platforms to encourage dialogue and feedback.	
Create Listening Sessions	• Create Listening Sessions where families can share their experiences and perspectives directly with educators and provide translators as needed.	

(Continued)

(Continued)

ENCOURAGE SELF-REFLECTION AND ASSET-BASED THINKING

Step	Actions	Identify next steps to support these actions in the context of your school or system
Embed Self-Reflection Activities in Meetings	• Include self-reflection activities during faculty meetings or professional learning communities, such as journaling or group discussions on implicit biases and assumptions.	
Promote Asset-Based Mindsets	• Promote an asset-based mindset by showcasing success stories of students and families who have overcome challenges, emphasizing their strengths and contributions.	

PROVIDE RESOURCES AND PROFESSIONAL LEARNING

Step	Actions	Identify next steps to support these actions in the context of your school or system
Ongoing Professional Learning	• Offer ongoing professional learning opportunities focused on addressing poverty, trauma, and the needs of multilingual or immigrant students.	
Create a Resource Hub	• Develop a resource hub for faculty and staff, including toolkits, articles, and access to community organizations supporting diverse student populations.	

(Continued)

(Continued)

	ESTABLISH SUPPORT SYSTEMS FOR FAMILIES	
Step	**Actions**	**Identify next steps to support these actions in the context of your school or system**
Connect Families to Services	• Identify and connect families to local social services for housing, healthcare, and employment assistance.	
Partner with Organizations within and Outside of Your System	• Partner with community centers or the district's multilingual services department to offer English as a Second Language (ESL) classes for families, boosting their confidence in engaging with the school.	
Provide Access to Resources	• Ensure families have access to essential school supplies through partnerships with local businesses or charitable organizations.	

CELEBRATE DIVERSITY		
Step	**Actions**	**Identify next steps to support these actions in the context of your school or system**
Host Cultural Events	• Host annual or quarterly cultural events where families can showcase their traditions through food, music, and storytelling.	
Mirror Student Diversity in the Curriculum	• Incorporate books, materials, and activities into the curriculum that reflect the cultural and linguistic backgrounds of your student population.	
Establish an Inclusion Council	• Establish an Inclusion Council to plan and oversee inclusive initiatives throughout the school year.	

(Continued)

(Continued)

BUILD TRUST OVER TIME		
Step	**Actions**	**Identify next steps to support these actions in the context of your school or system**
Create Expectations for a Compassionate Approach	• Train educators to adopt a compassionate and patient approach when working with families who may initially be hesitant to engage.	
Develop a Family Ambassador Program	• Develop a Family Ambassador Program powered by engaged families who mentor others to foster a welcoming and trusting school environment.	
Celebrate Milestones and Progress	• Create regular opportunities for celebrating milestones and progress, such as quarterly awards, family nights, and student showcases.	

Gauging the capacity of your team and available resources is important. Foster a sense of shared ownership by involving families, students, and educators in the planning and implementation of the plan. A solid foundation is more important than speed, so you may choose to begin with small, manageable initiatives and scale up as you build trust and confidence among the families and educators. Tracking progress through surveys, parent–teacher conferences, as well as academic and behavioral metrics to evaluate the effectiveness of the plan is key to holding all key players accountable and elevating the impact of the work. Moving toward family empowerment requires systemic commitment on the part of the school administration, school personnel, and the larger school community. To begin this systemic change, consider the steps outlined in Figure 1.1.

Figure 1.1

Four Steps to Systemic Family and Community Engagement

Step 1: Start With a Plan	Create a Plan of Action for . . .
	• Service-focused offices that provide information or orient families
	• Parent–teacher conferences
	• Informational meetings: Open House, etc.
	• Cultural activities and other celebrations
	• Community service projects
	• Identifying community allies: government, professionals, faith-based, business, first responders, etc.
	• Enhancing extracurricular activities
	• Establishing homework and academic assistance
	• Gaining knowledge about district services
	• Surveying community services and information
	• Eliciting, establishing, and assigning responsibilities

(Continued)

(Continued)

Step 2: Build Capacity so That School Staff Can Better Serve Families	**Build capacity for teachers, guidance counselors, and support personnel** on best practices, resources, and strategies for serving families with special needs and situations that affect the student. • Identify district offices to partner on engagement goals • Establish teams to serve families and the community • Equip office personnel to provide service and information • Identify goals and objectives (mission and vision) as a team • Provide personnel with training and access to information • Create a calendar to collaborate with pertinent contributors • Train personnel answering phones so that they are knowledgeable and know how to assist families in accessing credible sources
Step 3: Set up a Systemic Structure for Continued Improvement	**Establish a communication process for all involved parties:** community, families, students, and school staff. • Assign someone to keep the school website updated • Provide information on the website in students' languages • Provide easy access to teachers' emails (within two clicks on the school website) • Provide a weekly update regarding school events in a variety of formats (text, voice, app, website, fliers) covering essential announcements as well as school activities such as cultural, academic, extracurricular, and district events • Assign teams to reach out to families. Clarify when and how they should communicate, such as phone calls, emails, letters, etc.

	• Create and share a calendar of activities with families • Use social media strategically • Create systemic changes by analyzing data from ongoing communications, such as the best ways of reaching families and topics of greatest concern • Discuss ongoing topics and issues within the leadership team to reach solutions and continued improvement
Step 4: **Know Who We Serve: Community Mapping**	**Encourage families to join community groups** that address education as representatives or liaisons for the school, such as city councils and other government agencies. • Identify businesses, local organizations, government entities, school district offices, and community residents • Establish two-way discussions with community residents to establish topics of concern or interest • Conduct a survey to determine the most effective meeting setting (online, face-to-face, or a combination of both)

Source: Adapted from Figure 3.1 in Collado (2025).

Strategy 1: Self-Analysis Questions to Plan Your Actions

Strategy 1 sets the tone for a schoolwide self-analysis to clearly establish, with real data, how family and communities are partnering with the school. Consider the following self-reflection questions. What other questions should you ask to ensure that you are obtaining data specific to your school?

1. Does your school have a family and community engagement team to set goals, analyze family engagement needs, and establish appropriate goals and objectives?

(Continued)

(Continued)

2. What is in place to learn about the cultural representations of the community, such as the languages, traditions, and history of the school or community?

3. What training and capacity building are in place in your school to move families from involvement to engagement to empowerment?

4. What systemic changes can you make in your school to make families feel more invited to participate?

5. What barriers to engagement do families face in your school? What systemic changes can you make to remove those barriers?

6. What support structures can you put in place to allow faculty and staff to engage in self-analysis regarding their role in family empowerment? ●

When families, communities, and schools continually exchange information, students benefit because, together, all the institutions in their lives have established sustainable relationships and are able to intervene within their sphere (school) or in interactions with other spheres, such as family and community. Consider Strategy 2, which involves establishing collaborations to achieve the goal of schools and families working together within their respective spheres to benefit students.

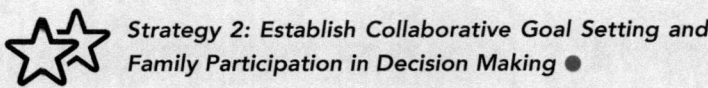

Strategy 2: Establish Collaborative Goal Setting and Family Participation in Decision Making ●

We connect with families so that, together, schools united with families can work to care for the whole child, from academic progress to social-emotional well-being. To fulfill this goal, it is critical for staff to create opportunities for families to be an active part of the process, including decision making. Identify families' strengths so you know who to tap for various roles. Find ways to collaborate with families—the more interactive the experiences are, the better. Learn how to engage families in respectful, culturally appropriate ways. Meeting families is essential to building a lasting partnership.

The establishment of a family and community partnership is a tide that raises all boats. Students feel more supported and feel more accountable academically and socioemotionally when they know that their families and the school are working collaboratively toward the same goals. Educators and staff become more aware of being service-oriented organizations, and families have a better understanding of their rights and responsibilities (Collado, 2008). According to Joyce Epstein and Steven Sheldon (2023), there are three spheres of influence in a child's life: family, school, and community. Schools that harness the potential of each sphere know how to integrate them and create a supportive structure of collaboration between families, school, and the community by strategically overlapping the spheres of influence (Epstein & Sheldon, 2023).

The Flamboyan Foundation has created a repository of resources on family empowerment. The repository provides tools to ensure that families are engaged and empowered in the academic process. The three stages of the process are as follows: a) attendance, b) content and delivery, and c) consistent, two-way communication. Each stage includes reflection questions and actions. We encourage you to explore these resources online at flamboyanfoundation.org (Flamboyan Foundation, 2023). For families to participate effectively in school community decision making, they must be well informed.

 ## Build Family Bonds With Frequent and Consistent Communication

When James S. Rickards Middle School in Fort Lauderdale, Florida, underwent a significant boundary redesign, incorporating a new section of the community into the school family for the first time, Principal Washington Collado recognized the need to take action to ensure that the new families felt welcome and more at ease in their new school. To help families adjust—the new and the old families—staff collaborated to produce the "Rickards Weekly Update," delivered in multiple languages and

(Continued)

various formats, including text, email, the district app, and voice. Rickards teamed up with the feeder school to provide families with the necessary information to ensure their students' success. The community began to rely on these friendly messages to maintain a sense of "knowing what is going on at the school." Because Principal Collado recorded the news himself, the community became familiar with his voice. It increased their level of trust in the administration, as well as in the knowledge that the school had implemented a plan to keep them well informed. Educators utilized the "Rickards Weekly Update" to highlight important dates and report cards, schedule family conferences, provide reminders for topic-based monthly meetings, share safety information, celebrate weekly accomplishments, make announcements about upcoming events, and convey critical information. ●

Inviting families to celebrate students' academic accomplishments (honor roll, most improved, character traits, and special awards) puts the school in a positive light and sets the tone for future conversations. If you put out weekly updates, make a point of sharing celebratory notes and accomplishments. Celebrate the accomplishments of teachers, groups, or individual students. Share news about the school community so that families can feel like participants in what happens at school. The relationships formed through consistent communication foster trust and create a setting for more positive and fruitful future interactions. Look beyond your school. Share celebrations, such as school events, awards won, sports team achievements, and teacher awards, with community leaders, businesspeople, civic and local organizations, and elected officials. Let families and the local community see your school succeeding. This lays the groundwork for inviting families and community members to participate in collaborative decision making at school.

ACTION STEPS

 For Developing a Goal-Setting Plan to Empower Family Feedback on School Improvement Plans

Phase 1: Establish a Collaborative Foundation

- Organize listening sessions with families to acknowledge past experiences and barriers to engagement.
- Provide family orientation programs to introduce the School Improvement Plan process and highlight its impact on student learning.
- Facilitate trust-building activities to create an inclusive space for dialogue and shared understanding.

Phase 2: Codesign Engagement Opportunities

- Create family advisory groups to participate in the development of initiatives within the School Improvement Plan.
- Create community input forums for families to express concerns, recommendations, and ideas for school improvement.
- Ensure family participation in curriculum discussions and goal-setting meetings to align their perspectives with educational priorities.

Phase 3: Strengthening Reciprocal Relationships

- Implement two-way communication channels such as digital surveys, focus groups, and structured feedback sessions.
- Schedule regular check-ins between educators and families to track progress on agreed-upon goals.
- Recognize and incorporate families' unique experiences and cultural knowledge into school improvement strategies.

Phase 4: Empowering Families Through Leadership Roles

- Provide leadership training for families to equip them with tools to participate in governance structures effectively.

(Continued)

(Continued)

- Encourage families to take leadership roles in School Advisory Committees and Multilingual Family Councils to contribute to school policies.
- Develop peer mentorship programs where experienced family leaders guide new participants in school decision making.

Phase 5: Allocate Resources to Support Collaboration

- Designate Family Liaisons to facilitate connections between families and school leadership.
- Establish accessible platforms for ongoing engagement, ensuring resources and updates are available in multiple languages.
- Secure funding for family engagement initiatives to ensure sustainable support structures.

Phase 6: Leverage Technology for Continuous Participation

- Utilize Canvas or similar platforms to host engagement modules and provide on-demand learning opportunities for families.
- Integrate interactive feedback tools such as virtual question and answer sessions and polling to enhance accessibility.
- Ensuring strong family–teacher relationships complements the use of technology to foster trust and inclusivity.

Phase 7: Measure Progress and Maintain Accountability

- Conduct annual evaluations to assess family feedback and engagement impact on school improvement.
- Review key performance indicators to measure effectiveness, such as participation rates and family-reported satisfaction.
- Adjust strategies based on ongoing reflection and feedback, ensuring adaptability to meet evolving family needs. ●

Strategy 2: Self-Analysis Questions to Plan Your Actions

1. List ways families are involved in the decision-making process at your school.

2. What school or district events are organized in collaboration with families?

3. How can you increase and improve the participation of families in your school and district?

4. What capacities does your school need from teachers, staff, and families to improve the quality of family partnerships?

5. What steps will your family and community engagement team take to reach out to families to learn how best to achieve this goal? ●

CHAPTER TAKEAWAYS

Effective family engagement must be intentional, culturally responsive, and context specific. This chapter calls on educators to take ownership for learning about the cultural and socioeconomic realities of the families they serve to build authentic, collaborative partnerships. Recognizing that many families—especially those from low-income or immigrant backgrounds—may face structural or emotional barriers to engaging with schools, this chapter underscores the importance of meeting families where they are. Schools must create welcoming and empowering experiences, building trust through consistent and meaningful engagement and communication. The success stories illustrate how shifting mindsets, honoring family histories, and leveraging community resources can lead to improved academic achievement and enhanced social-emotional well-being for students. Schools that prioritize inclusive, equity-driven family engagement strategies set the foundation for collective student success and encourage family participation and leadership.

- **Context-Specific Plans Matter:** Schools must design engagement plans rooted in the specific cultural, economic, and social realities of their communities.

(Continued)

(Continued)

- **Empathy Shifts Mindsets:** Educator training and direct engagement, such as home visits, help shift staff perceptions from judgment to understanding.

- **Family Leadership Is Powerful:** Schools should create leadership opportunities for families to advocate, guide, and contribute meaningfully to the school community.

- **Celebration Builds Connection:** Events that publicly recognize student and family success reinforce a shared culture of achievement and respect.

- **Systemic Structures Sustain Change:** Lasting family engagement requires institutional commitment, training, communication systems, and ongoing evaluation.

REFLECTIVE QUESTIONS

1. How can you enhance your school's mission statement to better reflect a commitment to family empowerment?

2. What specific leadership opportunities can we create for families to influence school decision making?

3. What structural or procedural changes do we need at the district or school level to ensure family engagement is a sustained, systemic practice?

OVERCOMING DEFICIT-BASED VIEWS

"Most family engagement initiatives are designed with a deficit-based lens, particularly those aimed at nondominant families defined as those impacted by systemic oppression, such as marginalization based on race, class, language, or immigration status." ●

—Karen L. Mapp and Eyal Bergman (2021)

Family engagement is recognized as a crucial aspect of student success and school improvement. However, even if unintentionally, most family engagement initiatives have been designed with a deficit-based lens, particularly when concerning families facing multiple societal obstacles based on racial discrimination, socioeconomic struggles, limited English proficiency, or immigration status. In many cases, deficit-based views are unintentional and rooted in societal biases and assumptions. Even well-intentioned efforts to involve families may inadvertently perpetuate inequalities and reinforce stereotypes. Schools may focus on what families lack in terms of resources, educational background, or English proficiency, without recognizing the wealth of knowledge, cultural values for education, and other valuable experiences they bring to the table. The impacts of deficit-based views are far reaching. Schools risk alienating families and caregivers, inadvertently undermining their potential contributions to their child's education. This can create a sense of exclusion and disempowerment among families, hindering their active participation. Furthermore, deficit-based views can perpetuate a cycle of low expectations and limited opportunities for families.

A paradigm shift is essential to overcome the challenges posed by deficit-based views. Educators must adopt an asset-based approach that acknowledges and celebrates the strengths and expertise of all families, regardless of their backgrounds. Authentic family empowerment involves recognizing families as equal partners in their children's education, valuing their input, and empowering them to play an active role in decision-making processes. The emerging paradigm demands a codesign model of collaboration, where educators and families collaboratively identify common obstacles and jointly create and execute enhanced educational experiences for children. Schools embracing the codesign approach comprehend the value of incorporating families' insights into solving challenges and problems.

Schools need to invest in professional development and training for educators to challenge biases, promote cultural competence, and cultivate authentic family partnerships. Ongoing dialogue with families can foster mutual trust and understanding, creating a collaborative and supportive learning community. By embracing an asset-based approach and recognizing the expertise of all families, schools can create authentic partnerships that empower students, bridge gaps, and pave the way for a more equitable and prosperous educational journey for all. Chapter 2 offers two strategies. The first (Strategy 3) provides guidance in overcoming deficit-based mindsets, and the second (Strategy 4) suggests action steps to utilize the assets, leadership skills, and potential that families bring to the table.

STRATEGY 3

Develop Strategies to Overcome Deficit-Based Mindsets ●

STRATEGY 4

Activate Families as Coeducators and Change Leaders ●

 **Strategy 3: Develop Strategies to Overcome Deficit-Based Mindsets ●**

The first step in developing effective strategies to overcome deficit-based thinking is to comprehend the challenges faced by nondominant families in the context of family engagement. Leaders need to explore the various forms of systemic oppression they encounter by analyzing how race, class, language, and immigration status affect school engagement. Understanding the complexities of systemic obstacles is essential for developing effective strategies to mitigate their impact and meet school goals. This approach also enables tailoring family engagement practices to the context-specific needs of families within your school community.

Families from low-income backgrounds, for example, may struggle to access essential resources and support, which can impact their ability to engage in their children's education actively. Economic disparities can also influence educational outcomes, perpetuating cycles of poverty. Families from marginalized racial backgrounds may face discrimination, stereotypes, and unequal access to educational opportunities. Immigrant families and those with limited English proficiency may encounter difficulties in communicating with educators and understanding school-related information. Language barriers can lead to feelings of isolation and exclusion, inhibiting meaningful participation in their children's educational journey. Immigration status poses yet another layer of obstacles for some families. Undocumented or immigrant families may face fear and uncertainty due to immigration policies, making it challenging to engage openly with schools. Fear of deportation or family separation can deter these families from actively participating in school-related activities. The compound effect of poverty, systemic racial discrimination, language barriers, and immigration status significantly hinders families' abilities to engage with school systems to ensure their child's success. It is not always easy for educators to thoroughly understand and acknowledge the complex challenges faced by families while also approaching them with an asset-based mindset. Sometimes these two realities might feel at odds with each other. But with persistence and commitment, it is indeed possible.

One of the primary challenges in transforming family engagement lies in overcoming resistance to change. Long-standing practices and traditions in education may be deeply ingrained, making it difficult for some members of the educational community to embrace a new, more inclusive approach. School administrators, educators, and even some families may be apprehensive about deviating from the status quo. Addressing this resistance requires clear communication about the benefits of inclusive family engagement and the positive impact it can have on student success and school improvement. Engaging in open dialogue, providing opportunities for input, and demonstrating the potential for positive outcomes can help build support for the transformation. Transforming family engagement often involves cultural shifts in how schools view and value families from diverse backgrounds. Educators may require professional development and training to enhance their cultural competence and sensitivity, thereby fostering a deeper understanding of the diverse perspectives and needs of families. Creating a culture of inclusivity requires ongoing efforts to challenge biases and stereotypes and promote an environment where families from all backgrounds feel welcome and valued.

ACTION STEPS

 For Overcoming Deficit-Based Mindsets

- ***Antibias Professional Development:*** Provide professional development that promotes cultural sensitivity and respect for differences and offers guidance for educators on how to reflect upon and explore unconscious bias. Ensure that educators and students understand how to challenge stereotypes and prejudices and how to foster an inclusive and respectful school culture.

- ***Culturally Responsive Professional Development:*** Invest in professional development on how to become proficient in culturally responsive practices that meet the needs of your particular student population. Topics should, at a minimum, cover how to practice culturally responsive communication, classroom management, behavior strategies, and curriculum design.

- ***Language Access:*** Break down language barriers by providing translation services and interpreters for school communications and school events.

- ***Equitable Resource Allocation:*** Bridge socioeconomic gaps by taking measures to provide families with the support they need. This may involve offering financial assistance for school-related expenses (yearbooks, uniforms, school dances, tickets to sporting events, or theatre productions). Ensure that families have access to educational materials and technology at home, such as school devices and Wi-Fi.

(Continued)

(Continued)

- **Provide Ongoing Guidance and Support:** To facilitate real change, professional learning experiences should be complemented with ongoing support and coaching from content experts. This ensures that the new mindsets are effectively incorporated into existing routines and practices.

- **Establish Senior-Level Positions for Family and Community Empowerment:** States and systems should invest in staff to elevate family engagement to a strategic level. Creating senior-level positions dedicated to family and community engagement demonstrates a commitment to authentic partnerships. In Denver Public Schools, Dr. Alex Marrero created the Chief of Student and Family Empowerment.

- **Develop Authentic Metrics to Track Improvement:** Establish policies that support a liberatory vision, ensuring *specific and measurable* expectations for improvement over time. Track that improvement over time and make course corrections in the plan based on data and feedback.

- **Incorporate Family Engagement into Teacher Evaluation Rubrics:** Policymakers should mandate family engagement coursework for all preservice teachers and include it in teacher evaluation rubrics. This commitment ensures that educators are well prepared to foster meaningful partnerships between families and schools. ●

Strategy 3: Self-Analysis Questions to Plan Your Actions

1. As you read this chapter, which unconscious biases surfaced for you? Consider what would make it easier and safer for you to explore your unconscious biases so that you can use that insight to plan professional development for your staff.

2. What common traps of deficit-based thinking did we miss in the chapter? How might you better address those issues in your school?

3. What examples can you think of from your own experience where families surprised you by exceeding your expectations? ●

⭐ Strategy 4: Activate Families as Coeducators and Change Leaders ●

Making the shift from deficit-based initiatives to asset-based initiatives is not easy. It requires school systems to relinquish some control, dismantle hierarchical structures, and embrace shared leadership—but it is essential. Deficit-based models must be rejected to avoid limiting the potential of authentic partnerships and to end harmful power imbalances between schools and communities. Asset-based plans require shifting to a mindset where families are recognized as coeducators, decision makers, and agents of change. Empowering families, particularly those from historically marginalized communities, means acknowledging that their cultural wealth, lived experience, and deep commitment to their children's success are valuable assets that the school would be wise to honor and utilize in the common endeavor to improve student achievement.

The assets families bring can contribute significantly to school improvement. Seek family input in shaping educational policies, curriculum development, and school improvement initiatives. Establish advisory committees and family leadership groups that enable families to actively participate in decision making and contribute their expertise. By acknowledging the valuable contributions of families, schools can cocreate a more equitable and inclusive educational experience, ultimately improving overall school outcomes. Schools need to make a commitment to move from low engagement toward family empowerment.

Low engagement is characterized by a lack of structure and consistency. Think of intermittent experiences such as Literacy and Math nights or ad hoc activities such as volunteering in the classroom or asking families to help with picture day and the School Book Fair as workers. Low-engagement strategies do not provide families with opportunities to be involved in decision making and leadership.

In contrast, *sustained engagement* has been proven to be more effective. This higher level of engagement requires an ongoing partnership between home and school. A reciprocal relationship between families and teachers includes a partnership in goal setting, providing timely assistance on how to support learning at home, and embedding the unique knowledge and experiences families bring into the academic areas of the school.

Family empowerment occurs through opportunities for meaningful decision making, such as codesigning family engagement opportunities, which provide families with decision-making rights and responsibilities (Dowd et al., 2017). To achieve family empowerment, schools must establish and execute a clearly defined family-empowerment process that aligns with and is incorporated into the school's mission and vision. Establishing and actively implementing a family-empowerment process will maximize families' knowledge of the schools and how they operate. This will lead to improved student academic achievement and social-emotional balance and will strengthen the culture of the school community and the broader community surrounding the school. The goal of this chapter is to offer alternatives to deficit-based views in family engagement initiatives, favoring strategies that lead to sustained engagement and family empowerment. To build a more equitable educational environment, the new normal must be founded on equity-driven practices rooted in social justice principles.

When schools activate families as coeducators and change leaders, they move beyond compliance-based engagement to liberatory partnership. This transformation centers on family voice, builds relational trust, and helps create schools where equity is not just an initiative—it is embedded in the way decisions are made and relationships are built.

A Mom's Journey from Frustration to Advocacy

Mrs. Feliz, a mother of two students at Information and Network Technology (IN-Tech) High School in the Bronx, New York, felt invisible at school events. As an immigrant parent with limited English proficiency, she attended meetings but rarely spoke, intimidated by the formal, fast-paced discussions. She wanted to support her children, but the language barrier and cultural differences made her feel like an outsider. Whenever she did muster the courage to ask questions, she received brief, surface-level responses that did not fully address her concerns. That changed when IN-Tech HS launched the Family Empowerment Initiative, a new effort to move beyond traditional involvement and give families a meaningful role in shaping school decisions. IN-Tech HS took the following steps to implement their Family Empowerment Initiative.

Step 1: Create an Inclusive Family Leadership Council

One of the first changes was the establishment of a Bilingual Family Leadership Council, which provided a structured platform for multilingual families to voice their concerns and cocreate solutions. At the first meeting, Mrs. Feliz hesitated to speak. However, when the facilitator, Principal Espinal, greeted her in Spanish and encouraged her participation, she felt an unexpected sense of belonging. "I have never been asked what I think about the school before," she admitted. By the third meeting, Mrs. Feliz coled a discussion on improving multilingual communication at the school, ensuring that translated materials were sent home in all major languages spoken by families.

Step 2: Meet Families Where They Are

Recognizing that many families like Mrs. Feliz felt more comfortable in familiar community spaces, the school moved its monthly family forums to local churches and community centers. Family attendance tripled, and families who had never set foot in a PTA meeting were actively engaged in

(Continued)

(Continued)

discussions about curriculum, student safety, and school policies. Mrs. Feliz became a trusted family liaison, helping other families navigate the school system. She even helped design a new Family Advocacy Workshop that educated families on their rights, resources, and how to speak up for their children.

Step 3: Move From Advocacy to Systemic Change

One evening, at a school board meeting, Mrs. Feliz stood up to address the district leadership. "We want the same things as any other parent—to see our children succeed, but we need schools to recognize our voices and value our experiences. Our engagement does not look the same as others, but that does not mean we do not care." The superintendent listened. A few months ater, the district adopted a policy requiring all schools to have multilingual family engagement plans.

Mrs. Feliz, once a silent observer, had become a leader not only in her school but also beyond. As she proudly watched her son walk across the stage at graduation, she knew she had helped change the system for families like her own. ●

"We want the same things as any other parent—to see our children succeed, but we need schools to recognize our voices and value our experiences. Our engagement does not look the same as others, but that does not mean we do not care."

FAMILY STORYTELLING

Consider other ways to invite families in as leaders and change agents in the school. One powerful example that we have seen make a difference is the deliberate creation of a space for family storytelling. Integrating family storytelling as a core part of school culture and instruction schools can affirm families as bearers of cultural wisdom, center their voices in the curriculum, and position families as essential contributors to student identity development and belonging.

What Family Storytelling Looks Like:

- Invite families to share personal, cultural, or community stories in classrooms or during school events.

- Incorporate storytelling into language arts, social studies, or heritage months.

- Facilitate intergenerational storytelling projects between students and their caregivers.

- Use stories as springboards for student writing, discussion, or performance.

- Ensure multilingual storytelling opportunities are available and celebrated.

Why Family Storytelling Works:

- It affirms students' identities and backgrounds as valuable assets.

- It counteracts deficit narratives by showcasing family strength, resilience, and wisdom.

- It builds empathy, cultural competence, and trust between educators and families.

- It creates two-way learning: families learn from school while schools learn from families.

 ## Centering Family Wisdom in the Classroom

Ms. Mirtha Aquino, a sixth-grade language arts teacher at Monte Cristi Middle School in the Washington Heights section of New York, recognized that conversations about equity often focused on what students needed but frequently overlooked the assets they brought. Acting in an asset-based mindset, Ms. Aquino created the Voices of Our Community curriculum unit, where students were invited to interview a family member about a formative experience. One student, Adlig-Marie, shared her grandmother's story of

(Continued)

(Continued)

fleeing civil war and rebuilding a life in a new country. Another, Arturo, told how his uncle taught him to fix bikes so he could help neighbors in their apartment complex. When families were invited to the unit's culminating Story Night. many showed up nervous, unsure if their family stories would be welcomed. However, as students stood proudly beside parents and grandparents, reading their narratives aloud, the cafeteria turned into a space of celebration and mutual learning.

Ms. Aquino noticed something shift. Families who had once avoided parent–teacher conferences now emailed to share memories or offer help. One parent said, "This is the first time I felt like the school wanted to learn *from* us." Monte Cristi's staff began incorporating storytelling in other areas—math lessons about budgeting became tied to real family experiences, and social studies classes included oral histories of migration, work, and resilience. What began as a writing assignment became a bridge between school and home, between generations, and between assumptions and truth. ●

ACTION STEPS

 ## For Activating Families as Coeducators and Change Leaders

- Reframe Family Engagement as Family Empowerment
- Train all school staff to adopt an asset-based mindset, viewing families as contributors of knowledge, not passive recipients of information.
    - o Organize a series of professional development workshops that focus on cultural competence in the classroom, where teachers hone their skills n creating an inclusive environment that respects and values the diverse cultural backgrounds of their students.
    - o Conduct workshops to help educators reflect on their unconscious biases. Engage them in activities and discussions to collaboratively gain insights into how biases can impact teaching and classroom interactions. Teach techniques to recognize and overcome these biases.

- Ask teachers to participate in a role-playing exercise where they encounter common classroom scenarios involving bias. Teachers then discuss how to recognize and respond to these situations in a way that promotes fairness and equity.

- Break Down Barriers to Engagement
  - Provide interpretation services, childcare, and flexible meeting times to increase accessibility.
  - Host family learning workshops to help families become experts in navigating the school system, understanding educational rights, and building advocacy skills.
  - Adopt a "meet families where they are" approach. Hold meetings in community centers, local libraries, churches, or apartment complexes to make it easier for families to feel welcome and invited as active participants.

- Ensure Ongoing, Two-Way Communication. Replace one-way communication (flyers, newsletters) with ongoing dialogue. Institute and systematize regular meetings between educators and families.
  - Create WhatsApp groups for classroom updates and conversations.
  - Host family coffee hours, Open Houses, and regular parent–teacher conferences.
  - Encourage attendance at virtual office hours for open questions.
  - Disseminate Pulse surveys to gather input on school climate and policies.
  - Implement systems for families to provide feedback on their child's education and their experiences with the school.
  - Act on family feedback and clearly communicate which changes were based on family input.

- Embed Family Empowerment into School Culture
  - Celebrate family leadership in school newsletters, social media, and public meetings.
  - Offer leadership development opportunities for families seeking to engage in district advocacy or policy reform.
  - Launch initiatives like Parent/Principal for a Day to demystify school operations and strengthen shared leadership.

(Continued)

(Continued)

- Celebrate the Cultural Wealth and Strengths Families Bring to the School Community.
  - Host events where families are encouraged to share aspects of their cultural backgrounds with educators and other families. This could involve food, music, storytelling, or art. One example might be a Cultural Potluck Dinner where families bring dishes from their cultural backgrounds to share. Educators and families can engage in conversations about their traditions, values, and experiences, fostering a sense of community. For example, educators and families can join forces to create a community garden on school grounds. Students learn about gardening, nutrition, and the importance of teamwork. Families and educators bond in an experience that respects the diverse talents of each participant.
  - Collaborate with your local community to organize community service projects and educational initiatives that benefit the school and the broader community.
- Create Leadership Roles for Families
  - Form Family Leadership Councils, where families help shape curriculum, school policies, and improvement plans.
  - Invite families to serve on hiring committees, ensuring representation in key staffing decisions.
  - Encourage student-led conferences, positioning families as active participants in goal setting and reflection.
  - Recognize Families as Coeducators. Move from a model where educators deliver information to one where families and educators cocreate learning experiences that are relevant, culturally responsive, and student centered. ●

Strategy 4: Self-Analysis Questions to Plan Your Actions

1. What barriers did Mrs. Feliz face in engaging with the school? How were they addressed? How would this play out at your school?

2. How did the shift from involvement to empowerment change her experience? How can your school improve in this area?

3. What role did the school play in ensuring families had real decision-making power?

4. What steps can your school take to create more inclusive leadership opportunities for families?

5. How can schools ensure that historically marginalized families feel valued and heard? ●

CHAPTER TAKEAWAYS

Transforming family–school partnerships by overcoming deficit-based views and embracing social justice principles is essential for creating an inclusive and equitable educational environment. Recognizing the strengths and expertise of all families, particularly those facing systemic obstacles, is crucial to fostering authentic and meaningful family engagement. Addressing deficit-based views requires a paradigm shift. We must move away from viewing family engagement as an add-on and recognize it as a core practice integral to student success and school improvement. Cultivating two-way communication, collaborative decision making, and equitable resources and support are key steps in empowering nondominant families as equal partners in their children's education. Embracing social justice principles is instrumental in dismantling systemic biases that perpetuate deficit-based views. Schools must adopt culturally responsive practices and prioritize family input in decision-making processes. By implementing the recommended strategies, educational institutions can create an environment where all families are seen, celebrated, and embraced as valued partners in their children's education.

(Continued)

(Continued)

- **Deficit-Based Views Are Widespread and Harmful:**
  Many traditional family engagement initiatives unconsciously operate from a deficit perspective, focusing on what nondominant families lack instead of valuing their cultural assets and lived experiences.

- **Systemic Obstacles Must Be Acknowledged and Addressed:**
  Race, class, language barriers, and immigration status compound challenges for historically marginalized families. Schools must actively address these systemic barriers.

- **Shift From Involvement to Empowerment:**
  Authentic partnerships require recognizing families as *coeducators* and *change leaders*, not just attendees of events. This includes giving families decision-making power and leadership roles.

- **Family Storytelling Builds Connection and Equity:**
  Integrating family narratives into the curriculum affirms identity, promotes cultural respect, and deepens relationships between home and school.

- **Asset-Based Mindsets Are Essential:**
  Educators must be trained to see families as knowledge holders and equal partners. Professional learning should focus on challenging biases and cultivating cultural competence.

- **Change Is Possible but Requires Intentional Investment:**
  Overcoming resistance, shifting school culture, and dismantling hierarchical structures require time, training, funding, and a commitment to leadership at all levels.

REFLECTIVE QUESTIONS

1. In what ways might your current family engagement practices unintentionally reflect a deficit-based approach, and how can these be reframed to highlight family assets?

2. How can your school create leadership pathways that genuinely empower historically marginalized families to shape decisions and policies?

3. What professional learning experiences are needed for your staff to recognize and challenge their own biases about families?

4. What systemic changes must be prioritized at your school or district to embed equity in family engagement practices?

ESTABLISHING TRUST FOR LASTING RELATIONSHIPS

> *"Teachers must get beyond the one-way communication activities we've relied on for so long and develop trust and mutual respect with the families we serve."* ●
>
> —Jamila Dugan (2022)

Families initiate a relationship with the school when they enroll their children. In doing so, families entrust the school to educate and nurture their children. Educators, in turn, accept the responsibility to ensure that the children progress in their learning and their developmental growth. Certain elements must be in place to build a positive, trusting, two-way relationship between schools and families. These include trust, a culturally rich and inclusive environment, as well as psychological and physical safety. To achieve this objective, we propose the following strategies:

STRATEGY 6

Establish a School Climate for Psychological and Physical Safety ●

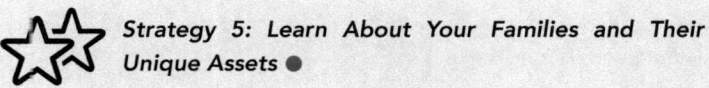

Strategy 5: Learn About Your Families and Their Unique Assets ●

There are many ways to learn about the families in your school community and their unique assets. Key strategies that have been seen to work well in schools include conducting a community scan, cultivating strong family–teacher relationships, celebrating the assets that families bring to the table, and getting to know the cultural perspectives of the families in your school.

CONDUCT A COMMUNITY SCAN

A community scan provides information about the families residing in the community, including their socioeconomic level, activities, and general needs. The scan collects information about businesses around the school, associations that may partner with the school, and city or other local government entities that share the common goal of serving the community, including faith-based organizations. When schools become familiar with the community they serve, they have the opportunity to introduce the community to the school and the school to the community. In his book *Empowering Family-Teacher Partnerships* (2013), Mick Coleman offers these strategies for conducting a community scan: drive or walk around the community, listen to local media (radio, television, newspapers), listen to underlying messages of conversation between families who visit the school, engage with local government entities and the chamber of commerce, and use the United Way social service (Coleman, 2013, p. 13).

Conducting a community scan is an ongoing activity that can be undertaken over time. It is not a one-and-done deal. Getting to know the local community assets around the school will provide valuable information that helps set the tone for building relationships with individual families and fostering a culture of trust throughout the school community. Community scans can (and should) happen as formal, explicit actions taken to gather information from key community entities. Additionally, information about the local community can be gathered on an ongoing basis by paying attention to emerging opportunities. For example, by creating a culture and environment where a member of your staff feels comfortable approaching you with a request from the community. Taking advantage of these serendipitous moments can go a long way toward building community rapport over time.

 **Doña Jilma—Tapping Community Allies for Partnership**

When Washington Collado became the principal at James S. Rickards Middle School in Fort Lauderdale, Florida, one of his primary goals was to become familiar with the entire community, especially given the boundary change that expanded the school's boundary area to include a wider number of students from areas of poverty. One of the support staff members working with English Language Learners became instrumental in promoting family engagement. Mrs. Jilma Cabral, whom the principal respectfully referred to as Doña Jilma, was heart and soul embedded in the community. She was familiar with the neighborhood and the priests at a local church that many families attended.

(Continued)

(Continued)

One day, prior to the end of his first year, Doña Jilma came into Principal Collado's office to advise him that the pastor wanted to meet with him and invite him to a dinner the church was providing for all graduating students who attended St. Clement Church. The dinner marked the beginning of a fulfilling and interactive relationship. Some of the school's poorest families attended the church. During Principal Collado's visit, he learned about ways the school could become more inclusive, including hiring more personnel who spoke Haitian Creole and Spanish. In the following months, church leaders participated in the school's multicultural festivals and teamed up with school staff to provide vital information regarding shelter and food resources to at-risk communities as a hurricane approached. The educators at the school also conducted family engagement training in the church, thereby expanding participation in parent–teacher conferences. ●

Most community residents are familiar with their local schools, and chances are that, in one way or another, they have a connection to the school. This is particularly true for schools that have been serving the same community for many years. Communities across the country have seen considerable changes in their socioeconomic and cultural makeup and dynamics. Groups of people move into the community, and other groups die off or move out. Schools also undergo regular changes in culture and composition when staff retire or leave the profession, move away or transfer to other positions, while new staff members join. These regular changes mean that schools and communities must continually make an effort to get to know one another.

When schools make an effort to understand their local community, they position themselves in a more advantageous position to seek collaborations and strategic partnerships as needed. As you conduct your community scan, learn about the key members of your community. We provide some practical suggestions here.

ACTION STEPS

For Conducting a
Community Scan

- Conduct community analysis to cultivate partnerships with other community residents.
- Identifying the neighborhoods where low-income families live is key to providing them with the resources they need.
- Find ways to partner with service-oriented organizations, such as the Lions Club, Kiwanis, fraternities and sororities, and professional organizations.
- Identify who the city officials are so you can invite them to school events.
- Identify local professionals and invite them to Career Day and professional fairs at the school.
- **Government offices, elected officials, and other public agencies** potentially have programs or information you can pass on to your school families so that they can benefit from the knowledge of these goods and services.
- **First responders, such as firefighters and police officers,** are key to maintaining a school's safety. Invite them to special events and orientations. Ensure they are familiar with the school's layout.
- **Faith-based organizations** are very often places where families and community members hold leadership roles in contrast to schools, where they might feel shy and do not engage. Sharing school information, such as cultural activities, amplifies the sentiment that the school is part of a broader network of community institutions.
- **Chambers of commerce, local professionals, and businesses** can partner with the school for special events such as Career Days. They can sponsor school events and teams. They can provide mentors and internships. ●

CULTIVATE STRONG
FAMILY–TEACHER RELATIONSHIPS

The relationship between educators and families is unique. There is, or should be, societal respect for the profession. Many cultures, including Hispanic and other cultures, manage this relationship with a self-imposed distance based on respect for the teacher's authority. These families acknowledge that, inherently, there is an institutional imbalance of power in the relationship between teachers and families. It is an imbalance of power accepted and respected by many families and cultures.

In economically disadvantaged communities, families are often not accustomed to advocating for themselves or their children, and many are uncomfortable pushing back when problems arise. Students who are learning English as a new language disproportionately contend with low or failing grades without intervention from their families. More often than not, families see the failing grades as the "fault" of the students. An imbalance of power also means that families gladly grant educators trust in their professionalism and the ability to educate and reprimand their children as necessary. Furthermore, studies consistently demonstrate a direct relationship between poverty, brain development, and academic achievement. A study conducted by a team of doctors and published in the *Journal of American Medical Associations* (*JAMA*) *Pediatrics* in 2015 showed conclusive evidence as follows: "Poverty is tied to structural differences in several areas of the brain associated with school readiness skills, with the largest influence observed among children from the poorest households" (Hair et al., 2015 p. 822). Schools that are sensitive to the inequities of students from low-SES families can implement family engagement strategies and other supportive measures to improve students' potential for success (Collado, 2025).

To cultivate a more fruitful and supportive relationship, Ari Gerzon-Kessler, Director of Family Partnership for the Valley School District (2019), proposes four pillars for promoting two-way relationships: *cultivating relationships, engaging in two-way communication, supporting learning and social-emotional well-being, and sharing decision-making and power.*

For educators, understanding how some families perceive their role in low SES communities is crucial information because it provides educators with options to implement and cultivate these relationships, thereby benefiting from interactions between the families and the school. These educators foster an asset-based mentality, where schools view families as partners who bring their cultural assets to the table in the relationship. We are proponents of developing healthy relationships by understanding the perspectives and lenses of families. Consider the following ideas:

ACTION STEPS

 For Cultivating Strong Family–Teacher Relationships

- Teachers can develop best practices for family engagement as a coordinated effort within their grade or subject area. This enables teachers to benefit from one another's experiences.

- Teachers can make a concerted effort to know the student's family and support system. This can be done by strategically using classroom exercises and basic student introductions.

- Teachers can reach out to families, preferably by phone, email, phone call, text, etc., to introduce themselves as teachers and discuss students' potential.

- Before contacting families, do your due diligence; get to know the student's personality, academic potential, and challenges. The key to the teacher–family relationship is to build on the student's potential and work toward their success.

- Begin the conversations by providing an opportunity for the family to say something about their child. Ideally, the conference's start will provide you with pertinent information about the family's lens and perspective on their child. The teacher can use this knowledge to build on it. Keep in mind that it is about building trust and fostering lasting relationships. ●

CELEBRATE THE ASSETS FAMILIES BRING

Families bring a wealth of assets to the school-family relationship, including, but not limited to, their love for their children, their desire to see them succeed, their willingness to collaborate with the school, and their efforts and time devoted to contributing to their children's success and well-being. Families also bring assets such as rich cultural traditions, languages, music, art, knowledge and expertise in various fields, and leadership skills. Asset-based schools incorporate families' assets into the fabric of school culture, making the culture stronger and more successful for the benefit of all.

Schools that do not operate on an asset-based model tend to blame families for their non-involvement (or perceived non-involvement). School personnel who engage in deficit-based thinking place all the responsibility for family engagement on families, rather than acknowledging that educators bear the primary responsibility for cultivating the relationships that lead to increased family involvement and participation.

Research findings indicate that family involvement contributes to both academic and social-emotional adjustments, as well as increased student participation in extracurricular activities (Hoglund et al., 2015). A causal relationship exists between family involvement and student conduct in school, in addition to other social benefits (Garbacz et al., 2017). Family involvement has a direct causal effect on students' aspirations to attend college or university (Watson et al., 2016). For all these reasons and more, cultivating positive relationships and discovering the assets families bring to the school community is essential in meeting school goals and ensuring student success.

ACTION STEPS

 **For Creating Activities
Built on Family Assets**

- Offer safety programs and events, teach families about the academic programs the school offers, help families learn about school processes, and offer classes on using technology.

- Find out what topics are in demand in your school community. Invite families to monthly meetings focused on topics of interest. When meetings are topic-based, families will attend to obtain information and have their questions answered.

- Host cultural celebrations. Celebrate cultural diversity as a strength to create a welcoming environment. Consult with the district and the office's multicultural division to determine what monthly celebrations or commemorations are in place and incorporate them into your school.

- Collaborate with community-based organizations that school families frequent, such as faith-based organizations, civic organizations, local fraternities, and sororities.

- Become an active community player by getting involved in local government and other offices that provide community services.

- Host academic fairs, poetry nights, art shows, and sporting events. Offer families a variety of opportunities to see their children shine. Make the learning that happens in school visible during these events. Invite families to lead the planning, organization, and execution of these events.

- Create opportunities for families to contribute, such as Career Day, volunteer opportunities, and weekend projects such as painting school murals or planting a garden. ●

For each of these activities, consider what assets your school families can contribute, and let them know that their contributions are welcome and celebrated.

GET TO KNOW FAMILIES' CULTURAL PERSPECTIVES

For schools and families, the process of getting to know each other involves understanding the lens through which each party (the family and the school) views its role in the relationship. Some families may maintain a respectful distance to avoid overstepping or interfering, keeping their distance out of fear of getting in the way. These families grant the school considerable trust, allowing it to act *in loco parentis*, a Latin phrase which means "in place of a parent." These families see teachers and administrators as second parents with the right to make (reasonable) academic and disciplinary decisions.

Some families, particularly those who do not speak English, might find the institution of school to be a confusing bureaucracy that is difficult to grasp and understand. Relating to their children's school may be a daunting and stressful endeavor. It is the responsibility of educators to understand the perspectives of families and address them in a manner that alleviates fears, provides necessary information in clear and understandable formats, and fosters a welcoming culture where families feel welcome and included. Ideally, outreach on the part of educators will lead to an alignment of perspectives where both families and educators operate with the understanding that family involvement in school is possible, desirable, and necessary for students' success.

Getting to know families, local organizations, and businesses presents the opportunity to create a strategic alignment of community and school goals. When this alignment occurs, educators, families, and students will potentially see the following results:

- Families and school personnel work together to meet the students' academic and socio-emotional needs.

- Families and teachers communicate and coordinate timely interventions to improve students' academic performance and achieve at a higher level.

- Participation increases during school events, volunteering, and on committees.

- Families feel empowered to communicate their difficulties when problems arise. They are aware of the channels for raising concerns and have the tools to work toward resolutions.

- Strategic planning improves students' futures.

- When issues arise, families have constructive dialogues with school staff and work to solve problems together.

- Families and schools plan collaboratively (and more effectively) to meet both long and short-term goals.

Consider the story of Principal Ernesto Calles from California. Sometimes, a relationship begins with a simple greeting.

 ### Principal Ernesto Calles— Breaking the Ice Starts With "Hello"

Cypress Elementary serves a low-income community in a district located approximately 80 miles east of Los Angeles, California. Although many families in the school may maintain a respectful distance, allowing the school to "do its job" without interference, this school leader has found a way of relating to the families. Principal Ernesto Calles makes small gestures each day in an effort to close this distance. He greets families and invites them to respond in kind. By initiating contact, he lessens their apprehension of overstepping. Most kids walk to school, either alone or accompanied by a family member (such as a parent or grandparent). With a blessing and a goodbye, they wish their children a good day. Principal Calles makes a commitment to stand at the gate each morning, accompanied by a few

(Continued)

(Continued)

teachers, to greet everyone. With a high five or a fist bump for the kids and an occasional hug, the principal has made it a tradition to be visible and approachable to the families every morning. He greets the families with a "Buenos Dias," or "good morning," or a comment about the child. This way, the principal opens the door to a relationship with the family. Families wait for their chance to greet the principal and offer their own comments. Proof that Principal Calles' invitation to engage is being warmly embraced.

Mr. Calles now serves another school in the same district, but the traditions and relationships with families he implemented have continued. At a recent Cypress School event, there were so many families that there was standing-room only. The school has decided to break up the events by grade and host them on different days to accommodate the increasing number of families wanting to participate. This growth in engagement began with breaking the ice, saying hello, and reaching out to start a lasting relationship with families and schools. ●

Families sometimes place principals and educators on a pedestal, feeling that initiating a conversation with them would be disrespectful. School leaders who commit to simple paradigm-changing practices begin the process of breaking down barriers and offer a foundation where a more profound relationship can be built.

ACTION STEPS

For Building Culturally Sensitive Family–School Relationships

- **Start with "hello":** As families and students arrive in the morning, Principal Calles greets them. Saying things like "nice haircut" or "your child is very smart," Principal Calles makes an effort to ease their shyness. Once families become accustomed to the principal's easygoing and inviting manner, they begin to seek out the hello, fist bump, or handshake.

- **Engage in conversation:** When families attend school events, their apprehension and nervousness are reduced by the informality of the event. This celebratory atmosphere is ideal for transitioning from a simple "hello" to a conversation with the principal, teachers, and other school personnel. Initiate conversations with families and encourage and train your staff to do the same.

- **Offer more opportunities:** Once a relationship has begun and families feel more comfortable, invite them to a parent–teacher conference and let them know about school events and other opportunities to get involved. Continue to build relationships.

- **Share calendar and ways of involvement:** Set up a table with families and staff who can communicate in the families' language and distribute calendars and other information. ●

Educators have various options for engaging families. These options become more apparent when the school, as an organization, looks to identify and become the family and community it serves. Understand their philosophy, who they are, whether students lack the necessary resources, and whether families experience anxiety when approaching the school.

Strategy 5: Self-Analysis Questions to Plan Your Actions

1. What are the socioeconomic, linguistic, and cultural demographics at your school?

2. How could you use a community scan to inform family and community engagement at your school?

3. What major celebrations occur in the community around cultural events and commemorating historical events?

4. In your school system, what do you do to learn about families' cultural perspectives and the assets they can potentially contribute to the school community? ●

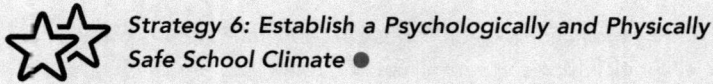

CREATE A SCHOOL ENVIRONMENT THAT LOOKS SAFE

When families discuss their children's school, they often mention how safe they feel it is for their children. The feeling of safety has several dynamics. When families see school shootings in the news, reports of bullying, and other unfortunate incidents, they start to wonder, "Is my school safe? Is my child safe?" Educators and staff can convey that they prioritize school safety in very visual ways. When families visit schools, they can see with their own eyes the essential elements that make a school safe:

ACTION STEPS

 For Attending to the Visual Elements of Order and Safety

- Create consistent processes and procedures: Families tend to associate disorganization with disorder, which makes them feel unsafe.
    - ○ Make sure morning and afternoon traffic patterns run smoothly.
    - ○ Provide clear signage for important rules and guidelines.
    - ○ Collaborate with district and local officials to analyze pick-up and drop-off traffic patterns.
    - ○ Determine the safest places for families to pick up students.
    - ○ Collect data on the patterns of students who walk to school and those who take the bus or drive themselves.
    - ○ Communicate pick-up and drop-off practices to families and follow up when procedures are not followed.

- Make sure that the school campus looks clean and well cared for.
  - The landscaping around the school is neat and well tended
  - Gardens are maintained
  - School common areas are clean and serviced regularly
  - Trash is not visible in common areas, and trash cans are emptied regularly
  - Buildings and school structures are clean and newly painted
  - Furniture is not out of place
- Establish a culture where school personnel are visible and readily accessible. They engage students, families, and fellow staff. Teachers greet students as they enter the classroom.
- Communicate safety processes and procedures regularly in clear language. Provide the procedures in multiple languages.
- Look for every opportunity, particularly at the start of the year, to introduce the school resource officer (SRO) to the community during orientation, open school nights, and other events where families visit the school. Ask the SRO to look for positive ways to interact with students and families to earn their trust. ●

CREATE A CLIMATE OF PSYCHOLOGICAL SAFETY

The national emphasis on treating undocumented immigrants as "criminals" by U.S. Immigration and Customs Enforcement (ICE) creates in children a fear that they, their families, or their friends will be deported, arrested, and harassed. This fear is very real. Children are listening to conversations at home, on the news, on social media, and on the playground. Schools should be a safe place for students to play, learn, and interact, free from harassment. School should be a safe haven, a refuge from the fears and anxieties that students sometimes experience outside of school.

In February 2025, an 11-year-old student from Texas committed suicide. According to news sources, she committed suicide after being taunted and harassed due to her family's immigration status. Students all over the country report fear and concern for immigrant families because of aggressive ICE activity. Their fears are not unwarranted. On Valentine's Day 2025, the official White House posted on its social media account @WhiteHouse, "Roses are red, violets are blue. Come here illegally, and we will deport you." These types of threatening messages are intentionally mean spirited. They are bullying tactics that contribute to students' feelings of fear and helplessness. The national discourse on "hunting down" undocumented immigrants and the taunting at school proved to be too much for this 11-year-old. It is imperative that schools seriously consider the effect that events and rhetoric outside the school can have on students. To counteract the anxiety that students experience outside of school, schools need to make a conscious effort to provide a safe haven for students where they can feel a sense of belonging, well-being, safety, and security.

Schools can create an all-hands-on-deck safety culture where the practices of SROs, police officers, crossing guards, and yard staff are all coordinated to ensure that students feel well cared for and protected. Families view orderly and hands-on processes as systemic efforts to keep their children safe. Seeing an SRO dialoging with kids makes students and families feel like the SRO is looking out for their best interests.

 ## Officer Joe—Building Trust One Relationship at a Time

SRO Joe Wright was assigned to serve at a middle school in an urban district of Broward County, Florida. This school serves families from low SES, which means more than 85% qualify for free and reduced lunch. Officer Joe, as the students and staff refer to him, finds that relating to students, staff, and families starts with visibility, being approachable, and earning the respect he demands by being a professional. Officer Joe begins his day in front of the school, where he talks to students, families, and staff and asks students about their progress in their classes. He knows who participates in the school band and who is on which sports team. Students trust him and often come to Officer Joe to discuss safety concerns when needed.

Officer Joe makes a practice of teaming up with teachers to create a leadership club composed of a diverse group of students, including those who require disciplinary reorientation. At the start of the year, he visits classrooms and is often seen talking to groups of kids or playing a sport, such as kickball or basketball. When families visit the school, he greets them kindly and professionally. He greets them in Spanish, which always brings a smile to the faces of the Spanish-speaking families.

Officer Joe is the first to respond and call for assistance during medical emergencies or other urgent situations that may arise. During emergencies, Officer Joe benefits from the respect and attention of everyone because he has built trust, established himself as a known presence, and is an ally to staff, students, and families. School staff and student families know that when a crisis occurs, they can count on Officer Joe to lead them to a safe outcome. ●

Officer Joe's hands-on approach to building trust enhances the psychological and physical safety of families and students. When crises occur, people are more likely to trust the actions and decisions of SRO Joe if they have a long-standing relationship with him built on trust.

TAKE ACTION TO ENSURE PSYCHOLOGICAL AND PHYSICAL SAFETY

 **Principal Martelli—Acting on Established Safety Protocols and Benefiting from Trust Deposits**

Virginia Martelli is an experienced principal who is respected and admired. She has been in service at George Washington Middle School in South Florida, for more than 15 years. One day, a father came to see her, visibly upset, due

(Continued)

to a fight that occurred after dismissal as the students were walking home. Principal Martelli paid close attention to the upset father, communicating that she understood his concerns and that appropriate individuals at the school would investigate the matter. To resolve the issue, she followed the established procedure to inquire about what had occurred and how the matter would be handled. Principal Martelli called over to one of the assistant principals and the student guidance counselor. After listening to the father, they advised the father of the steps that would be taken to get to the bottom of the situation and intervene accordingly to avoid further occurrences. Principal Martelli also promised to communicate with local authorities to arrange for additional patrols during dismissal. In a significant step that conveyed genuine concern, she asked the father how the student was doing. She invited the father to accompany the student to school the next day to prevent any further escalations. Principal Martelli offered what she had at his disposal, and the father understood and felt her sincerity. This was not the first time she had spoken to this father, and the father thought he could trust Principal Martelli and that the school would handle the situation. Because Principal Martelli had already established a relationship of trust, the safety process was well communicated, and school safety and administrative personnel were well known and introduced to the community, the father was inclined to trust that his concerns would be heard and that action would be taken to prevent further incidents of this kind. The principal could have dismissed this concern as a "community issue" because the students were not on school grounds and the incident did not occur on school property. However, Principal Martelli took steps to listen to the concerned parent and take immediate action because she knew that incidents in the community were likely to spill over into future incidents on school grounds. She also knew that if she had not acted quickly, all the efforts to build trust with this parent would have been wasted. ●

Principal Martelli benefited from the trust she had built in the school and the community. When difficult situations and conversations arise, what is in place at your school? Is there a protocol to ensure privacy? Does the protocol specify the right people to address when these issues arise? Does the school protocol include following up after the matter has been resolved? Following up is another important way of showing concern and making a "trust deposit."

As educators, we are not helpless. We must distinguish between what we can and cannot control. Then, we must act deliberately in the areas over which we have control with a vision, mission, and action plans (Collado, 2025). The first step is to establish the structure that will guide your actions, create a team, and take action. In the spirit of providing hands-on, practical interventions, we offer two distinct assessment tools: Assessment Tool A, which focuses on Safety, and Assessment Tool B, which addresses school climate. These assessment tools are suggestions, and by no means do they exhaust all the possibilities. As you go through them, apply your own school situation and particularities. For these plans to work effectively, they must be known and explained to families. In turn, the families can emphasize their importance from home.

ASSESSMENT TOOL A
Safety

Conducting a **school safety assessment** involves systematically evaluating potential risks and vulnerabilities within a school to ensure a safe environment for students, staff, and visitors.

1. *Assemble a School Safety Assessment Team*
   - The group should include school administrators, teachers, security personnel, maintenance staff, and possibly local law enforcement or safety experts.
   - Involve students and families for broader and multiperspective input.

2. *Identify Assessment Areas*
   - Physical Security: Entry points, fencing, surveillance, emergency exits, and lighting.
   - Policies and Procedures: Emergency response plans, visitor process, and bullying prevention.
   - Personnel Preparedness: Staff training, crisis drills, and response teams.
   - Student & Staff Well Being: Mental health, counseling services, conflict resolution programs.

(Continued)

(Continued)

3. *Conduct a Walkthrough and Inspection*
   - Evaluate building security: Doors, windows, locks, and access control systems.
   - Check surveillance systems: Cameras, alarms, and monitoring effectiveness.
   - Assess common areas for potential hazards: Playgrounds, cafeterias, and hallways.
   - Identify blind spots: Areas where supervision is limited with no cameras.

4. *Review Emergency Preparedness Plans*
   - Ensure fire drills, lockdown drills, and evacuation procedures are up to date.
   - Confirm emergency contacts and first-aid kits are updated and accessible.
   - Evaluate communication systems for alerting students, staff, and families.
   - Simulate emergency scenarios to test response effectiveness.

5. *Survey Students and Staff*
   - Conduct surveys to gather feedback on perceived safety concerns, including families
   - Assess bullying, harassment, and overall school climate.

6. *Identify and Prioritize Risks*
   - Review records of previous safety incidents, accidents, or threats.
   - Identify patterns and recurring issues.
   - Rank risks based on severity and likelihood.
   - Develop mitigation strategies for high-priority risks.

7. *Provide Recommendations and Develop an Action Plan*
   - Implement necessary upgrades (e.g., better lighting, security cameras).
   - Revise policies and improve training programs.
   - Address mental health resources and student support systems.

8. *Regularly Update and Reassess*
   - Conduct safety assessments at least annually or after major incidents.
   - Adjust plans based on new risks or community changes.

ASSESSMENT TOOL B
School Climate

Psychological and Socioemotional Safety

A school psychological and socioemotional safety assessment involves evaluating students' mental well-being, emotional support systems, and overall school climate.

1. **Define Objectives and Scope**
   - Determine the purpose (e.g., identifying bullying risks, assessing mental health support, improving school climate).
   - Define the population (students, teachers, families, staff).
   - Choose assessment tools (e.g., surveys, focus groups, interviews).

2. **Gather Data Through the Use of . . .**

   a) Surveys & Questionnaires

   Use vetted tools that are nationally recognized. Include questions on
   - Emotional safety (bullying, discrimination, peer relationships)
   - Psychological well-being (stress, anxiety, depression)
   - Teacher–student relationships
   - Access to mental health resources

   b) Interviews & Focus Groups
   - Conduct interviews with students, teachers, counselors, and families.
   - Ask about challenges, school culture, support mechanisms, and safety concerns.

   c) Observations
   - Observe classroom dynamics, peer interactions, and emotional expressions.
   - Assess physical spaces for safety and inclusivity.

3. **Analyze the Data**
   - Review disciplinary actions, counseling records, and reports of bullying or violence.
   - Identify trends, risk factors, and strengths.

(Continued)

(Continued)

- Compare findings across different student groups (age, gender, special needs, etc.).
- Use qualitative and quantitative methods for accuracy.

4. **Develop an Action Plan**
   - Address key issues found in the assessment.
   - Implement targeted interventions (e.g., antibullying programs, peer support groups).
   - Strengthen mental health services (e.g., more counselors, socioemotional learning curriculum).

5. **Monitor and Reassess**
   - Set benchmarks for improvement.
   - Conduct follow-up assessments periodically.
   - Adjust strategies based on new findings.

Strategy 6: Self-Analysis Questions to Plan Your Actions

- Begin the school day as if you were a parent. What does the morning and dismissal procedure look like from a parent's perspective? How orderly does it seem to families? How visible is the staff?

- How does your school share information about supportive structures for social and emotional assistance? How does your school communicate with families about strategies to address student anxiety?

- How can your school improve collaborative practices with the district, local police, and other local agencies regarding physical and psychological safety? ●

CHAPTER TAKEAWAYS

This chapter sets the tone for a crucial element in building a sustainable relationship: trust and a sense of safety. Schools do a better job of connecting with local communities when they are sensitive and cognizant of the socioeconomic and cultural dynamics of the community and strive to incorporate this cultural richness into the school's fabric. When schools celebrate students' cultures, students and families are more likely to experience psychological safety.

- **Trust Is Foundational to Family Engagement:** Building lasting relationships between schools and families begins with mutual trust, psychological and physical safety, and a culturally inclusive environment.

- **Community Scans Foster Asset-Based Relationships:** Conducting a community scan helps schools understand the surrounding community's strengths, needs, and resources. This knowledge enables schools to connect meaningfully with families and build partnerships with local organizations, faith institutions, and civic leaders.

- **Addressing Cultural Perspectives and Power Imbalances:** Many families, especially in low-SES or immigrant communities, perceive school authority with deference and may not feel empowered to advocate for their children. Educators must be culturally sensitive and intentional in creating opportunities for these families to engage and share their perspectives.

- **Promoting a Safe and Welcoming School Climate:** Safety is physical and psychological. Families feel more comfortable and involved when they see visible, orderly systems, friendly staff, and inclusive communication. A safe environment builds the foundation for trust and sustained engagement.

- **Leadership and Visibility Matter:** School leaders who are approachable, visible, and responsive—like Principal Calles and SRO Joe Wright—demonstrate that relationships are a priority. Simple gestures, such as greetings, active listening, and following up on concerns, can profoundly impact family–school trust and collaboration.

(Continued)

REFLECTIVE QUESTIONS

When schools engage in self-analysis, they can strengthen all types of processes and progress toward the goals and objectives they are expected to achieve. The following questions are designed to stimulate thought, self-reflection, and analysis. Consider these questions as an exercise of honest self-analysis:

1. How well do I understand the cultural, linguistic, and socioeconomic backgrounds of the families my school serves? In what ways have I used this knowledge to build trust and engagement?

2. Have we conducted a community scan or similar process to identify the assets and needs within our surrounding community? If not, what would be our first step to begin that process?

3. Does my school visibly demonstrate physical and psychological safety to families? What visual or procedural changes could further strengthen the perception of safety?

4. How do school leaders and staff model trust-building behaviors on a daily basis? Are there routines, traditions, or staff expectations that promote visibility, approachability, and family partnership?

BUILDING CAPACITY FOR AUTHENTIC PARTNERSHIP

> "Some people think they are in the community but in proximity. True community requires commitment and openness. It is a willingness to extend yourself to encounter and know the other." ●
>
> —David Spangler (n.d.)

Cultivating partnerships with families and communities involves understanding that different families and community residents may want to choose the way they can or want to partner with the school. This partnership will take three forms: involvement, engagement, and empowerment. The idea for educators and school leaders is to create the conditions and knowledge within families and organizations that enable them to exercise their preferred way of partnering with the school. This process involves educating families and organizations on how to become involved, engaged, and empowered, while highlighting the benefits to students and the school.

When schools deliberately seek to understand the community's dynamism and culture and look to open lines of communication, families will respond and take small steps initially. However, they will then take more assertive steps toward empowerment as they encounter a welcoming environment and a responsive school. Schools and districts that aim for robust family engagement strengthen family participation in three tiers: Tier 1 (Involvement), Tier 2 (Engagement), and Tier 3 (Empowerment).

Involving, engaging, and empowering families is one of the most effective steps schools can take to support students' long-term academic success. In a cross-analysis of 50 different studies, researchers found strong, long-term academic success as a result of this type of school–family relations (Michigan Department of Education, 2011).

The Three Tiers of Involvement

TIER 1—INVOLVEMENT

Involved families:

- ✓ Regularly consume school-provided communications regarding student progress and ongoing school activities
- ✓ Attend school events, volunteer when asked, and attend school meetings
- ✓ Set a conducive home environment for studying and help students with their homework

ACTION STEPS

 For Solidifying and Strengthening Family Involvement

- Be purposeful in providing constant information and get creative about different and more effective ways for teachers and families to communicate.
- Survey families to ask which languages they are most comfortable with.
- Use online options to facilitate parent–teacher conferences.
- Ensure the website is updated and families know how to access the website.
- Disseminate weekly bulletins via text (including WhatsApp), email, and voice.
- Provide families with correct and timely information.
- Utilize school major events, such as back-to-school orientations or other gatherings, to offer families information on how to increase their involvement.
- Ensure the school office provides information in the languages used in the community. ●

Involved families often have knowledge of the school's operational information but lack a comprehensive understanding of how schools operate. The next step is engagement, which involves exchanging ideas, responding to others, and actively participating in a two-way communication relationship with the school.

TIER 2—ENGAGEMENT

Engaged families:

✓ See the inner workings of the school's operations.

✓ Are active participants in school events, decision-making processes, and educational activities, as well as supporting programs such as arts, sports, or other extracurricular activities.

✓ Establish strong, positive relationships with teachers and staff.

✓ Collaborate with educators and other families to work toward common educational goals for students.

✓ Regularly provide input and feedback on school policies and practices.

✓ Initiate volunteering in classrooms, offices, and school events.

School personnel can provide students with the additional support these families offer as a result of family engagement. The transition from engagement to empowerment occurs when the engaged families are given a voice to take ownership of a project and are able to take the lead while following the school's interests and legal guidelines.

TIER 3—EMPOWERMENT

The ultimate goal of family empowerment is to transform families from passive recipients to active advocates in decision making (Hsiao et al., 2018). In the process of empowerment, schools help families feel confident that their voice matters and that they are being heard and invited to contribute to creating solutions. Prioritizing family empowerment helps to create the best possible learning environment for students.

Empowered Families:

- ✓ Are at the table where decisions are being made.
- ✓ Their input is valued.
- ✓ As partners, they have ownership of planning.
- ✓ Sit on district committees and have the authority to vote on projects and initiatives.
- ✓ Participate in staff interviews and personnel decisions.
- ✓ Offer feedback on budgetary decisions that involve capital projects such as remodeling or building new schools.
- ✓ Serve as active members on committees with authority to oversee school processes, including finances, inventory, and other operational practices.

Empowered families meet all the characteristics of involved families and engaged families and become decision makers together with the school. They may represent the school in district communities, advocate on behalf of the school, and use their voice to express their opinions and participate in enacting solutions. When educators cultivate family empowerment, it is a win–win.

ACTION STEPS

 For Solidifying and Strengthening Family Empowerment

- Provide families with the knowledge and skills they need to effectively support their children's education by hosting workshops, inviting guest speakers, providing literature, and offering training videos as resources.
- Take a cocreator approach to generating ideas. Conscientiously incorporate input from families.
- Equip families with the information and skills required to advocate for their children's needs within the educational system.
- Involve families in decision-making processes that affect their children's education, reinforcing their role as key players.
- Remove barriers so that more families can participate. ●

In addition to emphasizing that family and community engagement plans must address each tier of family participation (involvement, engagement, and empowerment), this chapter provides specific guidance on implementing systemic supports to help more families transition from passive recipients of school information to school and community leaders in their own right. To begin this endeavor, we suggest schools meet families where they are by creating spaces of engagement in the places where they feel most comfortable (Strategy 7). Once engaged, we recommend offering families structured supports in the form of family leadership training institutes to help them hone their leadership skills and put them into practice in the school setting and beyond (Strategy 8).

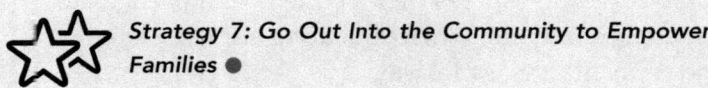

Strategy 7: Go Out Into the Community to Empower Families ●

The research on family and school systems that genuinely empower families is limited. This is particularly true for schools serving families in low socioeconomic neighborhoods. It is rare for this type of collaboration and partnership to occur because it requires the administrator to be comfortable relinquishing some of their power and authority.

The following vignette illustrates how Principal Camaj successfully implemented systemic changes to empower families by meeting them where they were to engage them in conversation in an open, transparent way—bringing the school to families, using that feedback to create further forms of engagement that were flexible and culturally responsive, and then implementing more systemic practices to move families from engagement to empowerment. The vignette illustrates that with the right action plan and follow-through, schools can ensure that families who were once silent observers become active voices in shaping the school's future.

Three Essential Ingredients for Meaningful Engagement

At DeWitt Clinton High School in the Bronx, New York, there were constant struggles with low family engagement. Parent–teacher conferences had low attendance, and school events rarely saw more than a handful of families. The school's administration, led by Principal Martini Camaj, recognized that they needed a different approach—one that not only invited families into the school but also actively met them where they were and empowered them in the process.

Determined to move from traditional involvement to authentic engagement and empowerment, Mr. Camaj and his team launched a bold initiative: *Los Tres Golpes Con El Director*.

This new engagement model, inspired by the Dominican breakfast known as *Los Tres Golpes*—which consists of mangu (mashed plantains), queso frito (fried cheese), and salami—was designed to nourish, strengthen, and sustain relationships between families and the school. Each meeting focused on three essential "ingredients" for meaningful engagement:

- Ingredient 1: Information & Transparency: Sharing critical updates and resources in an accessible, culturally responsive way.
- Ingredient 2: Dialogue & Partnership: Creating two-way conversations where families share their concerns, aspirations, and ideas.
- Ingredient 3: Action & Empowerment: Providing families with concrete roles and opportunities to shape school policies and decisions.

Instead of expecting families to come to the school, Principal Camaj and his team took *Los Tres Golpes* directly to the community to strengthen families' confidence in getting involved.

Step 1: Bringing the School to Families

One afternoon, families in a predominantly Dominican and Latino neighborhood gathered at Doña Carmen's Café, a small but lively restaurant known for its mangu and café con leche. They were there for the very first *Los Tres Golpes con el Director* session.

As families settled in with plates of traditional Dominican breakfast, Principal Camaj greeted them warmly. He spoke in English and Spanish, making sure every family member felt included. "*Hoy estamos aquí para hacer lo que hacemos mejor en nuestra cultura–comer juntos y hablar juntos*," he said (We are here today to do what we do best in our culture—eat together and talk together). Rather than presenting a long list of school policies, Mr. Camaj started with a simple question: "What do you want for your children's education?"

Families, some of whom had never spoken directly with a school leader, initially hesitated. However, as the discussion progressed, they began to

(Continued)

(Continued)

open up. One mother, Vera, shared that she never attended school herself and often felt intimidated when visiting. Another father, Miguel, explained that he worked two jobs and struggled to keep up with his daughter's grades. Listening intently, Mr. Camaj reassured them: "*La escuela no puede hacer esto sola. Necesitamos que ustedes sean parte del equipo. Pero también entendemos que necesitamos facilitarlo para ustedes*" (The school cannot do this alone. We need you to be part of the team. But we also understand that we need to make it easier for you).

Step 2: Flexible & Culturally Responsive Engagement

From the feedback at that first meeting, DeWitt Clinton High School implemented new engagement pathways:

✓ School in Your Neighborhood meetings at local barbershops, laundromats, and churches, so families did not have to travel to the school.

✓ A WhatsApp group for direct communication with teachers and administration, making it easier for families to ask questions.

✓ Family advocates, trained by the school to serve as liaisons, help bridge gaps for families who feel disconnected.

✓ Evening and weekend family workshops for working families, covering topics like college readiness, financial aid, and accessing student grades online.

One parent, Fatima, a refugee from Syria, had never attended a school event before. However, when a multilingual staff member personally invited her to a WhatsApp orientation, she agreed to join. Within weeks, she felt confident enough to attend a School Advisory Council meeting, where she shared ideas on how to support multilingual families.

Step 3: From Engagement to Empowerment

As families grew more engaged, their role in school decision making increased. *Los Tres Golpes* was no longer just about attending meetings; it was about leading change.

• A family-led advocacy group successfully lobbied for multilingual counselors to better support families of emerging multilingual students.

• Families collaborated with the school board to introduce a career mentorship program that connected students with local professionals.

- Families helped shape new policies on homework expectations and grading transparency, ensuring families had a voice in academic decisions.

One of the biggest victories came when families successfully advocated for free evening English language classes at the school. This empowered families to build their language skills and better support their children's education.

At the end of the school year, Principal Camaj stood before a packed cafeteria—not for a traditional school meeting, but for a celebration of family–school partnerships. Families who had once been silent observers were now active voices in shaping the school's future.

As he looked at the crowd, he smiled and said: *"Cuando empezamos, muchos me preguntaban qué era Los Tres Golpes en la educación. Ahora, ustedes son la respuesta. Son el sazón, la energía, y la fuerza de nuestra comunidad escolar"* (When we started, many asked me what 'Los Tres Golpes' meant in education. Now, you are the answer. You are the seasoning, the energy, and the strength of our school community). And as the families cheered, they knew this was just the beginning. ●

The benefits of shifting from family passivity to family empowerment are profound for schools and families. Families have unique skills, perspectives, and experiences that will enrich the nuances of schools. When schools intentionally involve families as partners, they invest by relying on the expertise of the people who know their students' needs better than anyone else. This can lead to academic and social-emotional goals that are better tailored to a student's unique needs (Angell et al., 2016).

It takes confidence and leadership to cultivate and actively seek out empowered families. It can be disconcerting to have members of your decision-making team who do not report directly to school-sanctioned authorities and who operate with greater independence than school personnel. It is not easy to honor all voices and perspectives, especially when those voices might be voices of dissent. However, the pay-off can make an unforgettable difference in the lives of families and students who are often ignored by the system. The following Action Steps provide guidance to move from involvement to engagement to empowerment.

ACTION STEPS

 For Progressing from Involvement to Engagement to Empowerment

....

LEVEL	DEFINITION	KEY ACTIONS FOR SCHOOLS	EXAMPLE TOOLS/ STRATEGIES
Involvement	Families participate in one-way communication activities (e.g., receiving updates or attending events without active input)	• Share timely, transparent information • Ensure communication is culturally inclusive	• Create multilingual family newsletters and fliers • Host parent–teacher conferences
Engagement	Families participate in two-way communication with schools, sharing feedback and collaborating on small-scale initiatives	• Host flexible events tailored to family needs • Facilitate culturally responsive conversations • Create opportunities for dialogue	• Meet families at their convenience during neighborhood events • Post on social media groups for direct communication • Provide family liaisons
Empowerment	Families lead and cocreate decisions, policies, and initiatives that shape the school community	• Assign decision-making roles to families • Provide training and tools to support active participation • Foster systemic, sustainable partnerships	• Sustain family advisory councils • Facilitate family workshops (academic support, leadership training) • Create advocacy groups lobbying for systemic improvements

Strategy 7: Self-Analysis Questions to Plan Your Actions

1. If you had to guess, what percentage of families in your school would you say fall into Tier 1 (Involvement), Tier 2 (Engagement), or Tier 3 (Empowerment)? What steps can you start taking now to move families up to a higher tier?

2. Who do you know in your local community who could help you organize a family meeting in a location outside of school? Who on your staff do you know who could help you come up with a catchy promotional hook that would be familiar to families, pique their interest, and encourage them to attend?

3. What can you do in your school to create a space where more families can exercise their leadership skills for the benefit of the school and the community? ●

 **Strategy 8: Offer Leadership Training for Families ●**

FAMILY LEADERSHIP INSTITUTE

Retired Lieutenant Colonel Consuelo Castillo Kickbusch is a fierce advocate for immigrant students and families. Consuelo (as she prefers to be called) created the Family Leadership Institute (FLI). The FLI is an educational program that empowers families to support their children by providing the knowledge, tools, and support they need to grow as leaders. The cornerstone of the program is supporting family leadership to enhance student success in school and life (Castillo Kickbusch, 2023).

In addition to supporting family empowerment in home and school partnerships, districts implementing FLI are committed to "producing a cadre of knowledgeable and committed families and caregivers who actively support school and community efforts to benefit their children and encourage other families to do the same" (Castillo Kickbusch, 2023, n.p.). The robust curriculum includes modules and experiences that enable families to understand the past while looking to the future, incorporating cultural and generational perspectives, literacy through family history, education as a key to a better future, facing challenges, college field trip experiences, and improving family and school relationships.

The following vignette exemplifies the power of implementing the FLI as a foundation of what became family empowerment. These families provided an example of resiliency, growth, responsibility, and leadership despite their challenges, not only for their children but for the entire community.

 ## From Empowerment to Leadership: Families Leading for Change

Mrs. Naira Alvira, the Bilingual Community Liaison of the School District of Osceola County, Florida, is a well-respected authority on family engagement, particularly for multilingual and immigrant families. Trained in the implementation of FLI, she was eager to offer the program to the families in her district. Her poise and expertise in delivering the modules captivated the families' attention, and her warmth and dedication won their hearts.

Unfortunately, two months prior to the completion of the yearlong FLI program, the world came to a screeching halt in March 2020. The families did not want to stop the sessions. In record time, FLI's first online module was created. Through the interactive virtual module, FLI provided a family action plan that outlined vision, goals, and responsibilities, along with related actions. The plan included communication, problem solving, advocacy strategies, resources, individual leadership, and responsibility. The lessons proved to be invaluable to the families' success as they were now navigating extra-academic responsibilities throughout the pandemic.

Through their perseverance, the families completed the yearlong FLI program.

To honor their new leadership skills, the Multicultural Education Department engaged families in the planning process for the graduation ceremony. The proud graduates of the FLI program wanted to celebrate their accomplishment and hard work alongside their families and the families of their fellow graduates. They also knew that it was essential to have a graduation celebration that would serve as an inspiration to other families, motivating them to join the next cohort of FLI participants. Because a traditional graduation ceremony was out of the question, the planning team organized a celebratory and joyful Drive-in Graduation.

On graduation day, each family car received pizza boxes, drinks, and a program outlining the ceremony. From the comfort of their car, they could tune in to the designated radio station and hear the ceremony. A giant outdoor movie screen projected the prerecorded program. The presentation included a photo of each FLI graduate, culturally inclusive videos, and a family empowerment session on how to engage with schools and advocate for their children. They were also able to compete for prizes by using a cell phone to call in answers to questions. Winners flashed their lights while prizes were delivered to their vehicles. Honking horns replaced the traditional clapping. The pilot was so successful that, five years later, over 150 families participate in the FLI program.

The program graduates challenged themselves to create modules specific to the district's families' lived experiences. With the assistance of the Multicultural Education Department and under the leadership of Mrs. Alvira, the Empowered Families Institute (EFI) was created. The family leaders set their own path in their leadership journey by taking an active role in contributing to the EFI programming and promoting it with other families at regional school sites.

Some of the graduates took on leadership positions in the Emergent Bilingual Parent Leadership Council. This district-wide family council weighs in on the support the district provides ESOL students and their families. The Council brings concerns and recommendations to the superintendent to work with the leadership team. The families' ability to identify common areas of success and areas of opportunity to ensure the best support for families across the district is inspiring and impressive. ●

Although the FLI's programming provided targeted strategies and support for family engagement, it was the families' input that resulted in the EFI, which truly encapsulated the spirit and power of family empowerment. As families participated and contributed to the modules, families began to exert their leadership in communicating with their children's teachers and administrators. The family's presence, participation, and contribution in school leadership and decision-making groups, such as the School Advisory Committee (SAC) and Parent–Teacher Organization, underscored the value of empowering families as leaders.

SCHOOL ADVISORY COMMITTEES

The SAC is state sanctioned for every school. It requires families to share responsibility by providing input to the school's budget, voting for the use of school improvement funds, and cocreating the school improvement plan. These are core initiatives toward school improvement and weigh heavily in the success of the school. All FLI and EFI parent graduates went on to actively participate in their children's school SAC committees, ensuring language supports for multilingual learners, acculturation efforts for immigrant students, and culturally responsive celebrations that celebrated all nationalities. These actions led to an inclusive environment for all students, as evidenced by favorable student climate surveys and an increase in learning gains. Not only did the families use their voices to advocate for change, but they were also part of the decision making that worked toward improving the education and well-being of all students.

TRAINING FAMILY LIAISONS

Family Liaisons are school staff members whose primary role is to act as advocates or outreach contacts for families within the school system. Including a family empowerment component in professional learning for school personnel was important. A large school district elected to utilize Title I funds to staff a Family Liaison at all its Title I schools. On-demand training was created as modules on the Canvas platform for family liaisons.

A component of the training involved creating a two-way communication approach, where families and family liaisons provided feedback to strengthen the training continually. Families have felt welcomed and trusted that their feedback was valuable to the school. Canvas and other technologies serve as tools for family empowerment; however, they are most effective when supported by strong family–teacher relationships.

Honoring the families' knowledge and lived experience was key to building family self-efficacy. This provided families with the courage to speak their truth, allowing the school to match resources to the families' needs better. Creating connections between families and schools via the SACs and Multicultural Family Councils was essential to strengthening the family–school connection. The measure of a true partnership is an evidenced organizational system that provides families and schools with training, resources, authentic engagement, trust, and respect, allowing each partner to contribute to the conditions for meaningful learning.

Consider the suggested actions below to implement system strategies. These strategies will promote collaborative goal setting and allow family participation in decision making.

ACTION STEPS

 For Fostering a Leadership Environment for Families

- Codesign engagement opportunities that allow families to participate in the design of initiatives such as the School Improvement Plan.

- Create reciprocal relationships that encourage mutual communication between educators and families through partnering on setting academic goals and embedding the families' unique experiences and knowledge into school initiatives.

(Continued)

(Continued)

- Provide training and resources to empower families to participate in leadership roles in established school organizations such as the SAC and Multilingual Family Councils to build confidence in contributing to school governance.

- Allocate resources such as Family Liaisons to support family–school collaboration.

- Leverage technology platforms to provide continuous and engaging learning for families while balancing technology-based tools with strong family–teacher relationships for effective participation.

- Encourage family feedback in multiple forms (in person, via phone, letters, email, and digital spaces) to ensure accessibility. ●

Strategy 8: Self-Analysis Questions to Plan Your Actions

- In what ways did the families' contributions to Empowered Families Institute modules and advocacy strategies reflect their growth as leaders in the community?

- How can other districts replicate the success of programs like FLI and Empowered Families Institute to engage families in culturally diverse communities?

- What systemic changes might be necessary to sustain and expand such programs on a larger scale?

- What partnerships (e.g., with community organizations, local businesses, or government agencies) could enhance the scalability of these programs?

- What evaluation tools can be used to measure the success of the program?

- How can districts ensure that family leadership councils, like the Emergent Bilingual Parent Leadership Council, remain effective and aligned with local needs?

- What mechanisms can be implemented to maintain program sustainability after initial funding or leadership transitions? ●

CHAPTER TAKEAWAYS

Chapter 4 emphasizes that authentic school–family partnerships require moving beyond superficial involvement to intentional strategies that foster empowerment. Building these partnerships involves recognizing the diverse ways families wish to connect with schools and creating systemic conditions that support all three tiers—Involvement, Engagement, and Empowerment. Through culturally responsive outreach, leadership training such as the FLI, and opportunities for shared decision making, families can transition from passive recipients of information to empowered cocreators of school initiatives. Providing this guidance and systemic support is particularly crucial in communities that have been historically marginalized or underrepresented in school decision making. Schools that prioritize transparency, collaboration, and respect for family expertise create sustainable models of partnership that boost academic success and strengthen the fabric of school communities.

- **Three-Tiered Partnership Model:** School engagement plans should include strategies for supporting families at each tier of participation: Involvement (receiving information), Engagement (participating and collaborating), and Empowerment (coleading decision-making processes).

- **Culturally Responsive Strategies:** Schools must meet families where they are—linguistically, geographically, and culturally—using community-based events and platforms to increase accessibility and trust.

- **Family Leadership Institute (FLI):** Programs like FLI build families' capacity for leadership through culturally grounded, strengths-based curricula, enabling families to support their children and their communities.

- **Empowered Families Institute (EFI):** Empowered families can lead family advocacy initiatives and decision-making councils.

- **Systemic Change Through Voice and Action:** Families' active participation in shaping school policy, contributing feedback, and leading initiatives demonstrates the value of shifting power dynamics toward equitable collaboration.

- **Sustainable Structures for Empowerment:** Districts can foster authentic partnerships by investing in structures like family liaisons, multilingual resources, leadership councils, and training modules codeveloped with families.

(Continued)

(Continued)

REFLECTIVE QUESTIONS

1. What systems or practices are in place to ensure that families, especially those from marginalized backgrounds, have a genuine voice in school decision making?

2. In what ways can we adapt our communication and engagement strategies to reflect the cultural, linguistic, and logistical realities of our school community?

3. How can we build family leadership capacity in a way that not only empowers families but also sustains long-term collaboration and shared governance?

4. What are the barriers (structural, relational, or attitudinal) preventing families from moving from engagement to empowerment, and how can we begin to dismantle them?

BUILDING LASTING COMMUNITY PARTNERSHIPS

> "The fact is that it takes more than the school to educate a student. It takes a city. It takes a community that can provide support from the parks department, health services, law enforcement, social services, after-school programs, non-profit (organizations), businesses, and churches." ●
>
> —Mick Coleman (2013)

As we travel to and from work, we may pass through the community without knowing or conscientiously realizing the people, businesses, and organizations that make communities come to life. H. Richard Milner IV (2020) succinctly states, "Communities are deeply rich in human capital—regardless of zip code. However, educators in some schools may struggle to understand how to build on the many talents and assets of the community—perhaps because in order to recognize and acknowledge expertise in the community, we, as educators, must see the brilliance of the students with whom we work" (p. 93).

In Chapter 1, we covered how educators can craft context-specific family–school engagement plans. In Chapter 3, we discussed the importance of getting to know families and building trust to foster lasting relationships between schools and families. In Chapter 4, we shared ways in which educators can meet families where they are and increase their role. In Chapter 5, we venture outside school walls and discuss ways educators can harness the power of their communities for the mutual benefit of the community and the school. When schools deliberately look for ways to celebrate and integrate the community into the school and the school into the fabric of the community, schools have the potential to be constructive contributors to the community's economic, social, spiritual, and cultural growth. The strategies in Chapter 5 explore ways schools can enhance their value in the community, foster trust within it, and contribute to a genuine sense of communal life. Strategy 9 provides guidance on building partnerships with community partners, and Strategy 10 examines ways to maintain, enhance, and strengthen these partnerships.

STRATEGY 9

Build Partnerships with Community Partners ●

STRATEGY 10

Maintain, Enhance, and Strengthen Partnerships with Community Partners ●

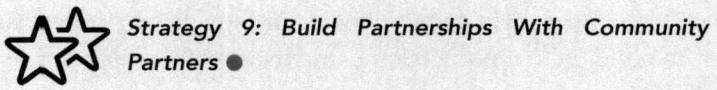

Strategy 9: Build Partnerships With Community Partners ●

SOLICIT FEEDBACK AND ACT ON COMMUNITY FEEDBACK

Mick Coleman (2013) made the point that communities are defined not only by a geographic location but also by "the quality of life it provides through its institutions" (p. 11). When we refer to the community, we are referring to several possible definitions that encompass the physical surroundings of the school, including the city, town, and county. However, in urban settings, students may come from different parts of the district rather than one consolidated neighborhood. When we use the term *community* in this book, we refer to the community of families whose children attend the school or who have historical, cultural, and community ties to the school. Schools cannot operate in a vacuum isolated from the families, organizations, elected officials, and civic entities that positively impact school life with their partnership.

The following story showcases how seriously the school took its mandate to solicit feedback from the community and to then act on that feedback. It also highlights the numerous benefits that result from partnering with community members, paying attention to the assets they share, and drawing upon those assets for future projects.

 ## The Power of Community Partnership

Dr. Washington Collado was excited about his new assignment as principal to a new middle school in the city of Oakland Park, Florida. Realizing he was not familiar with the community and its school boundary, he printed a map of the school boundary. After scanning the community, it became evident that the school mainly served families from modest socioeconomic means. Within the school boundaries, families were living in mobile homes, low-income housing, and middle-class homes. Families brought a rich diversity of cultures, religions, backgrounds, and traditions, mainly including Latinos, Haitians, African Americans, and Anglos. This cultural diversity was a source of pride among the staff. These educators recognized the need to engage all families and local community organizations as active participants, thereby giving them greater ownership of their roles within the school.

As part of the community scan and relationship-building process, the principal met with various groups, including leaders of organizations and family groups. One of the parents, respectfully yet assertively, commented

(Continued)

(Continued)

on how the school's unkempt gardens and poor conditions of the school grounds affected their perception of the school. Consciously or unconsciously, families made assumptions based on the school's exterior appearance and what was happening inside the classrooms.

This well-intentioned feedback from a key sector of the community required attention and appropriate action. Here was an opportunity to build trust. Families, students, teachers, and staff teamed up to plan a school beautification project. More than 50 people took part in the beautification event. Using information from the community scan, school personnel visited local stores and, with the support of families and businesses, purchased plants, mulch, and flowers. On the day of the event, students, families, and teachers were divided into teams and assigned a task. The participation of the School Board member, the city mayor, and two city commissioners was welcomed because the news of their participation provided an opportunity to take the message of openness and collaboration back to their offices. The school facility service team was glad to be part of the action and appreciated the team spirit.

As the families and volunteers worked alongside the school's teachers and staff, conversations ensued, and they got to know each other better. Some families, many from modest financial means, brought their landscaping tools and were ecstatic to be part of the fun. One parent invited Principal Collado to his church and introduced him to a church family group. A mother advised an assistant principal that her husband was a police officer who could partner up with the school as needed. A science teacher at the school shared that she was part of Alpha Kappa Alpha. This service-oriented organization welcomed opportunities to provide community service. The school proudly welcomed the opportunity and established a strong relationship with the local chapter, which led to several creative projects, including health fairs, future beautification initiatives, and events celebrating Black History.

With one simple project, the school staff increased their awareness of the community's willingness to support the school. The improved appearance of the school provided a daily visual reminder for students and families that the school was taking action to make them feel more welcome. The community embraced school as much as the school embraced the community. It was a visual sign of change and a harbinger of good things to come. ●

TAKE STEPS TO MEET THE COMMUNITY

Noguera et al. (2012) discuss the invisibility of specific Black and brown communities. To combat that invisibility, they offer the following deliberate actions:

- *Get to know the community*

- *Envision, plan, and align strategic partnerships*

- *Identify community resources*

- *Celebrate traditions and the community's cultural heritage*

How can school leaders develop a plan to ensure that school staff are knowledgeable about the surrounding community? In many schools, the staff live outside the school boundaries. However, the fact that educators may not live in the communities they serve does not necessarily mean that they are unknowledgeable about the community's life, families, and important dynamics.

As we discussed in Chapter 1, devising a plan to learn about the community must come from an asset-based mindset, which looks for ways to identify potential partners, identify vulnerable populations, and coordinate the potential for aligning resources to improve community life. Joyce Epstein and Sheldon's (2023) body of work on community engagement refers to the overlapping spheres of influence in children's learning: family, community, and school. These three overlapping spheres shape the life of students. When these spheres experience limitations, the student experiences them as well. The greater the interrelations among these overlapping spheres, the greater the possibility for support for students, as these institutions can work in tandem with one another.

To start discovering the community, schools can begin by conscientiously and deliberately learning about the community, including the different neighborhoods where students come from, and the housing structures in those neighborhoods.

Consider a school in areas prone to natural phenomena: tornadoes, fires, hurricanes, snowstorms, and other types of storms that require coordinated attention and communication. Schools can serve as a great point of improving safety messages, proactive preparedness, or other necessities of coordinated services. The following is a story based on actual events and a result of the benefit of knowing the school's community.

 ## The School as a Community Resource in Times of Crisis

In Florida, when schools close due to incoming hurricanes, schools serve as family shelters for dangerous storms. Some schools are designated as medically equipped shelters, whereas others are pet-friendly shelters.

A school serving the Fort Lauderdale area had been cultivating a positive relationship with the community and building strong relationships. These efforts were embedded naturally into all types of planning at the school. During hurricane season, a potentially deadly storm was aiming straight for South Florida, and all schools were ordered closed. One of the staff members, who worked very closely with a local church and was a reliable partner to this school, realized that some of the poorest residents lived in a trailer park community just north of the school. Almost all the residents in the trailer community spoke only Spanish. The staff member was concerned that they may not know how the shelter process works. School staff also knew that many of these houses had poor or no access to reliable Internet, an essential tool for keeping track of in-the-moment emergency information. In a joint effort, church volunteers and school personnel visited the trailer park community to distribute informational flyers written in Spanish about the shelter process. The coordination between the community and the school reflected their mutual desire to ensure the safety and welfare of the community in a life-threatening situation. ●

This strategic partnership, as exemplified by the relationship between a church and a school, can be leveraged to serve other purposes. It is to the advantage of schools to become familiar with community institutions and to align their goals for mutual benefit. Schools that invest time and human resources in identifying and cultivating strategic relations with other community members and organizations can maximize the services and educational support they obtain from these agencies and organizations. Indeed, developing these relationships with other community actors can draw positive attention to the school. It can also allow students, families, and community members to see the school as the hub or center of community life and information. The term *community actor* refers to all individuals who share and act on behalf of the community, including children, parents, grandparents, businesspeople, elected officials, police officers, firefighters, professionals, and others.

IDENTIFY COMMUNITY RESOURCES

When schools identify community resources, they can make them available for families. Communities often offer sports and arts programs, libraries, city-sponsored events, and health services. Community professionals can be identified and invited to become part of the school's excitement. When community leaders are invited to speak to students, particularly in low-income communities and communities of color, they offer students a concrete visual representation of the careers they can aspire to. Ideally, this motivates students to remain focused and committed to working hard to achieve academic success. Consider inviting a diverse range of professionals, including businesspeople, service-oriented professionals, local elected officials, and representatives from state and federal agencies. Take, for example, Officer Frank, a community police officer, who made an indelible impact at a school.

 ## Teaming With Community Actors to Build Community Pride

On a daily basis, Officer Frank St. Louis could be seen at James S. Rickards Middle School, his assigned school in Broward County, Florida, striking up conversations with students, inquiring about their grades, and giving them high-fives. He also organized a school leadership program, The Cadets Club, a club that taught students service-oriented leadership. As a U.S. Army veteran with a heart for service, Officer Frank sought other ways to build community with students.

Together, Officer Frank and Principal Washington Collado discussed a project they would eventually call "In Gratitude, We Salute." On a November night, between Veterans Day and Thanksgiving, the school's Cadets Club, teachers, staff, and the Parent–Teacher Student Organization, with the unwavering support of the community, hosted a dinner for community servants at the school. The invitees included community first responders, firefighters, police officers, medical personnel, and veterans related to students and staff. The principal wrote a special invitation letter and hand-delivered it to the Police Chief and Fire Chiefs. More than 30 gladly participated. The event allowed teachers and students to interact with great public servants who, in turn, got to meet some great students.

Other projects included health fairs and school beautification projects, which drew participation from school board members, police officers, local business leaders, families, and city officials. The city mayor smiled as he worked alongside the students, the school board members, and the teachers. Everyone who participated was left with a special feeling toward Rickards Middle. ●

ACTION STEPS

 For Building Partnerships With Community Organizations

· ·

- Identify community organizations and partners
- Become knowledgeable of the services they provide and consider how these services can be of benefit to the school families (many families may not know these services exist)

- Invite local community organizations and government officials to celebrate with the school

- Invite community partners to Open House so that they can let the school community know about the resources they provide

- Identify ways of creating partnerships with service-oriented organizations and bring those services to the school ●

Strategy 9: Self-Analysis Questions to Plan Your Actions

1. Has your school leadership conducted a community survey of local organizations with which the school can collaborate? If not, what resources would you need to gather that information?

2. In what ways can your school do a better job of soliciting feedback from key community actors and acting on that feedback in ways that mutually benefit the school and community?

3. What events can you organize, or steps can you take, to enhance community relationships? What additional steps can you take to meet more members of the community around your school?

4. Who on your staff is best positioned to team up with families and community members to identify community resources and bring those resources to your school families? ●

In Strategy 9, we discussed ways to relate to and establish bonds with community actors, cultivate partnerships, and benefit from their contributions and goodwill to serve the needs of the school community, including students, teachers, and staff. Now, we introduce our readers to Strategy 10, which discusses how schools can maintain and enhance strong bonds with community partners.

Strategy 10: Maintain, Enhance, and Strengthen Bonds and Partnerships With Community Partners ●

CELEBRATE COMMUNITY CULTURAL HERITAGE

One way to maintain, enhance, and strengthen bonds and partnerships with community partners is to get to know the major cultural groups in the area and, as a school, actively participate in integrating that cultural heritage into the curriculum and celebrating those heritages through school events. Doing so shows the outside community and school families that you value their cultural heritage and see it as an asset to the school, as well as a source of pride. This makes families and community members feel that the school is actively making efforts to build lasting partnerships and relationships between the community and the school.

As part of their efforts to deepen their connection and relationship with the community, many schools around that country host a yearly multicultural celebration during Hispanic Heritage Month. The celebration features music, choreographed folkloric dances, food (which is a must), and an art exhibit. Hundreds of families are always in attendance. Some wear the traditional colors of their country of birth, whereas others wear red, white, and blue. The conversations, applause, and gauzy looks of pride are evident. A multicultural celebration is an excellent and joyful way for community members to learn about each other's various cultural dress, music, practices, food, and histories.

Videos and photographs of the event included recordings of bands, dances, performances, paintings, costumes, food, and other signs of celebration. The photos and videos often found their way into other countries and states. They were shared among the local community as participants proudly shared how their culture was being celebrated at school. Another example of a school–community celebration involved a partnership between the Omega Psi Phi Fraternity and the school to showcase the contributions of African Americans to the local community.

 # Show Students That You Take Pride in Their Cultural History

At James S. Rickards Middle School in Fort Lauderdale, Florida, one administrator and several teachers and staff members were members of the Omega Psi Phi Fraternity. Omega Psi Phi is a historically African American fraternity founded more than 100 years ago at Howard University. More than 250,000 men have been initiated into Omega Psi Phi Fraternity, Inc. The fraternity members are committed to meeting the needs of African Americans in the areas of health, housing, civil rights, and education.

In partnership with this community organization, the school invited Omega Psi Phi members to organize an event showcasing an educational display at the school that would educate the school community regarding the special contributions African Americans have made to U.S. history. The display was set up in the school media center.

From trials and tribulations to triumphs and victories, the media center evolved into a documentary featuring memorabilia from African American history. The team, comprising educators, business leaders, and active and retired individuals, was designed to foster a collaborative effort between school community members and local community members.

The fraternity brothers organized themselves into different stations, where they would interact with students on various topics. Teachers brought classes to the media center at a scheduled time to interact with the gentlemen from Omega Psi Phi who were proudly wearing the organization's colors. The gentlemen were engaging, patient, and knowledgeable. I took pleasure in attending every class period.

One particular boy, a student, observed the scene without saying a word. When Principal Collado asked what he thought about the exhibit, his eyes welled up, and he said, "I am just very proud of these men." That became one of those educational moments Principal Collado will never forget. ●

TAKE STEPS FOR THE COMMUNITY
TO KNOW YOUR SCHOOL

In addition to celebrating the cultural heritage of your local community, another way to maintain, enhance, and strengthen partnerships with community partners is to ensure that the community is aware of your school. Whether outreach efforts involve the accomplishments and celebrations of the school or how the school can serve as a vital resource for communities (in times of crises for example), it is important to be strategic about ensuring the community knows what is going on in the school academically, in extracurricular activities, and in students' and families' engagement opportunities. For effective engagement to occur, schools must do more than offer one-way attempts to "inform" the community. When schools invite families or community members for sit-and-get meetings without taking the opportunity to engage, it serves a limited purpose. For our families and communities to know our school and its dynamics, schools must be deliberate about introducing themselves to the community in interactive ways.

- *Communicate clearly and frequently using multiple forms of communication including multi-media. Create a system that fosters interactive communication.*

- *Showcase learning activities.*

- *Celebrate your school's accomplishments.*

- *Make sure community members know what resources are available at the school during times of crisis.*

ACTION STEPS

▶ **For Maintaining, Enhancing, and Strengthening Bonds and Partnerships With Community Partners**

• •

- *Invite Community Members Into Your School:* During Open House or other traditional events, invite key community members to learn about safety protocols, procedures for drop off and pick up. Ensure that these meetings include a two-way dialogue. Dialogue ensures that questions and concerns are validated and addressed.

- *Address Topics of Concern to Families and Community Members:* During monthly meetings, such as councils and family–teacher associations, address themes and topics that are prevalent in the minds of community members and families. Invite special guests, such as school reform officers, district officials, and safety officers, to lead these efforts in engaging and dialoging with families. Remember the vital word: *conversation.* This is an opportunity for listening and speaking. Inviting community members to come in as experts on topics of concern to families and community members opens up a two-way partnership that further strengthens school and community relationships.

- *Use Effective Means of Communication:* To establish communication and provide information in the appropriate language, get to know families' language limitations. Furthermore, take time to understand the families' philosophical views of involvement in school. Consider teaming up with local and community organizations that attract families, such as faith-based organizations and other groups.

- *Draw on Community Assets:* Build relations with elected officials, councilmembers, the police department, the health department, and emergency response teams. Invite them to be special guests in school meetings. ●

Strategy 10: Self-Analysis Questions to Plan Your Actions

1. What cultural or historical events does your local community observe? How does your school integrate these cultural practices into the curriculum, school events, and culture of the school?

2. What steps can you take to partner with key community players who do not yet know your school?

3. What allies in the community can you partner up with for collaborative projects that will mutually benefit the school and the community?

4. What systemic practices are in place to learn about the concerns of community members and act on them as appropriate? ●

CHAPTER TAKEAWAYS

This chapter explores how schools can form authentic, lasting partnerships with their surrounding communities. It emphasizes that genuine community engagement is built on commitment, openness, and mutual respect. Educators are encouraged to see and harness the often-overlooked brilliance and assets within their communities. Through inclusive efforts, strategic partnerships, and recognition of diverse cultural heritages, schools can become trusted hubs of community life that reflect and uplift the families they serve.

- **Authentic Community Engagement Requires Intentionality:** Educators must build trusting, reciprocal relationships with community members through deliberate outreach and inclusion.

- **Recognize the Rich Assets of Your Community:** Every community holds human capital, culture, and institutional support that schools can partner with to benefit students.

- **Seek Out Strategic Partnerships to Multiply Impact:** By aligning with local organizations, faith groups, city officials, and service providers, schools can expand support systems for students and staff.

- **Celebrate Community Culture and Identity:** Showcasing traditions, cultural events, and local contributions fosters pride, validates student identity, and strengthens bonds between schools and families.

- **Give the Community the Opportunity to Know Your School:** Through transparent communication, showcasing accomplishments, and educating families, schools earn trust and support from community members.

REFLECTIVE QUESTIONS

1. In what ways does your school actively introduce itself to the community?

2. What local organizations or individuals could become powerful allies in your school's mission?

3. How do current school activities reflect (or fail to reflect) the diversity of the families and communities you serve?

4. How can your school redesign events to be more interactive, inclusive, culturally affirming, and community focused?

STRENGTHENING STUDENTS' ACADEMIC POTENTIAL: EMPOWERING FAMILIES WITH PRACTICAL WAYS TO PROVIDE SUPPORT

"Making intentional efforts to create partnerships with families who are most at-risk, raising their voices, and expanding their opportunities to be engaged in their student learning, is a way to ensure that every child has the opportunity to thrive." ●

—National Association for Family, School, and Community Engagement (2023)

Empowering family and community members to be active contributors and collaborators in education is critical to the academic and social-emotional growth of the students and the success of the community. In this chapter, we acknowledge the challenges families face in advocating for their children's academic growth while also acknowledging the assets they can draw on to support students' academic success. We offer guidance on drawing on families' existing capacity and suggest tools and strategies to help families grow their capacity, enabling them to become even more empowered as academic coaches who can accelerate student achievement.

STRATEGY 11

Build the Capacity of Families to Support Academics ●

STRATEGY 12

Align Family and School Support to Boost Students' Academic Achievement ●

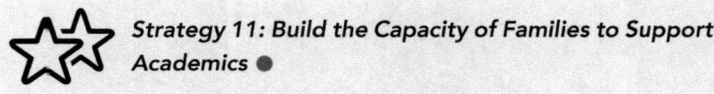 **Strategy 11: Build the Capacity of Families to Support Academics ●**

TRUST AND HUMAN CONNECTION COME FIRST

We have discussed several reasons why families may not feel welcome or part of the school community. The reasons are complex and unique to each family's experience. The one certainty is that to support family empowerment successfully, educators must engage in laying a solid, culturally responsive foundation of trust. Empowering families by honoring their contributions and creating interactive forums for them to share with one another is essential for systemic and sustainable student academic achievement and socioemotional success.

Trust is everything. It begins with the first interaction, which typically starts with front office personnel. Even when families approach with only hand gestures to convey their message, office staff should be skilled at "listening" patiently before acting on unwarranted assumptions. Ideally, the family would be introduced to a team member who understands their language. Regardless, all families who approach the school should be greeted by welcoming staff who are practiced in offering a human connection, whatever that may look like. On the journey to academic success, school staff (from office personnel to classroom teachers) must work as partners with families—that partnership begins with a warm welcome, inviting families in as valued members of the school community.

The following story illustrates how, unfortunately, non-English-speaking families often do not receive a warm welcome in school offices. Staff do not always take the time necessary to assess their own needs or how school or district resources can be utilized to serve those needs. However, with careful interventions, school cultures can change, staff can be trained in welcoming practices, and structures can be established to ensure that valuable resources are well known and easily accessible.

 **Create a Structure of Support**

Marta Pizarro arrived in central Florida from Guatemala with two children: a son in middle school and a daughter in elementary school. Although the neighboring elementary school enrolled her daughter, the middle school would not enroll her son because the family could not provide proof of vaccinations. The school referred Señora Pizarro to the health department. There were several problems with this request: she did not have sufficient command of English to navigate the process, had no means of transportation, and was unsure of how to get to the health department or what to do once she arrived. Sadly, the result was that the boy stayed home for the rest of the school year.

The following academic year, the middle school again denied the student enrollment, this time because he was overage. Auria Lopez, the

(Continued)

(Continued)

school's ESOL educational specialist, was at the front desk that day and, coincidentally, overheard the conversation. Ms. Lopez referred Señora Pizarro to the Multicultural Education Department. The executive director of the Multicultural Education Department was able to step in to ensure that the registration process was equitable, fair, and in compliance with the law. Working with the middle school, members of the Multicultural Education Department were able to teach Señora Pizarro her rights, help her develop her language skills, and provide her with sufficient knowledge of the system to serve her son's needs, ensuring that she could exercise her decision-making parental rights regarding her son's education.

Due to the teamwork between Ms. Lopez and the team at the Multicultural Education Department, Señora Pizarro was able to learn her rights and enroll her son the next day. A social worker from the district was able to assist her with the necessary paperwork, as well as connect the family to vital community resources.

Following this incident, the middle school saw the need to improve its practices so that in the future, when families arrived with special needs, the staff would be better equipped to provide families with the guidance and support necessary to meet students' academic needs. The Multicultural Education Department provided the school with guidance and training to meet the needs of vulnerable families. The collective effort between the district, school, and family led to a bridge of trust between the family and the school as well as a structure to serve vulnerable students in the future. ●

Families send educators the very best they have—their children. These are their treasures, and we must build and nurture trust with families as a foundation, first and foremost, before we can begin to work on academic goals. With trust as a foundation, building capacity for families to serve as academic supports at home becomes possible.

When schools take a deliberate approach to meeting families where they are without negative judgment and look to build upon families' assets collaboratively, great things happen for students. The following vignette illustrates how school efforts to invite families in and provide them with tools to become more involved and engaged can help build their capacity to support their children academically, socially, and emotionally.

 **Building Capacity at School and at Home**

For years, Xochitl Carranza had felt disconnected from her son's education. She trusted that his teachers knew best, but she rarely attended school meetings or parent–teacher conferences, convinced that her role was to ensure he completed his homework. However, as eighth grade approached, she noticed his grades slipping, and he seemed increasingly frustrated with schoolwork.

One afternoon, Xochitl received a message from Rocky Mountain Middle School in Denver, Colorado, inviting families to a workshop "Building a Study-Friendly Home: Supporting Academic Success." The workshop, part of the school's new initiative on "Family Engagement for Increased Home Academic Support," promised to offer practical strategies for families to create a structured learning environment at home. Intrigued, Xochitl decided to attend.

At the workshop, the school's Parent Coordinator (Family Support Liaison), Ms. LePlatt, greeted families warmly. The session emphasized three key areas:

1. Creating a structured study space at home
2. Using technology effectively to monitor progress and communicate with teachers
3. Setting academic expectations and routines that reinforce learning

Xochitl listened as Ms. LePlatt explained that students perform better when families provide structure and support, even if they do not personally understand the subject matter. A multilingual teacher demonstrated how families could use the district's online grade portal to check assignments

(Continued)

(Continued)

and communicate with teachers. Another parent shared how setting up a "homework hour" each night helped their child stay on track.

Determined to take action, Xochitl went home that evening and talked with her son. They agreed to set up a quiet study space in the corner of their cramped living space, away from distractions. They also developed a plan: each evening, before dinner, she would sit with him to review his assignments, ask about his day, and check his school's parent portal. She even practiced sending an email to his math teacher, something she had never done before.

Within weeks, Xochitl noticed a change. Her son became more organized, and his frustration decreased. One day, he came home excited to share that he had scored a B+ on a math quiz. "Ma, I think it's helping," he admitted. Encouraged, Xochitl attended another workshop on helping students set academic goals.

By the end of the semester, Xochitl was no longer just an observer in her son's education. She had become actively engaged in supporting his academic success. She even encouraged other Spanish-speaking families to attend future workshops, knowing firsthand the difference it could make. ●

In addition to becoming active on the school campus and in school activities, family engagement involves families providing students with academic support at home. The school can strengthen families' capacity to give this home support through ongoing communication regarding academic needs and by ensuring that two-way communication channels between teachers and families are robust and regularly frequented. When their family is involved, students feel a greater sense of responsibility and accountability. The same applies to schools—schools feel a greater sense of responsibility and accountability toward meeting students' academic goals when families are involved.

ACTION STEPS

 For Building the Capacity of Families to Support Academics

••

Schools Can

- Offer family workshops on how to support academics at home.
- Provide guidance and instructions on how to access online student portals showing grades and missing assignments.
- Encourage families to advocate for their children by making sure they know who to contact with questions about grades and who to go to when they have questions about assignments.
- Ensure there is a family representative on the family and community engagement team.
- Instruct teachers to discuss students' academic progress with them during class.
- Ensure that students have access to technology and a reliable Internet connection.
- Provide Wi-Fi resources for families who might not have Internet access at home.

Families Can

- Establish a study-friendly atmosphere.
- Create a designated space for studying where students can organize their supplies and study materials.
- Provide homework assistance while fostering student autonomy and independence.
- Communicate the message that the student is ultimately responsible for learning and completing quality work.
- Communicate family expectations to their children.
- Enforce designated study times and routines that ensure academic success.
- Log on to the school website and parent portals to monitor their child's progress.
- Know how to communicate with teachers regarding missing work, falling grades, or help with assignments. ●

ACTIVITY

Create a Plan to Build the Capacity of Families to Support Academics

Step	Guiding Question	To educate families on what is required to support students academically	To provide families with the infrastructure they need to support students at home
Step 1	What is your plan?		
Step 2	How will you systemically build capacity for your staff?		
	How will you help build capacity for families?		
Step 3	What systems will you put in place?		
	How will you ensure continuous improvement?		
Step 4	What steps will your family and community engagement team take to reach out to families to learn how best to achieve this goal?		

Strategy 11: Self-Analysis Questions to Plan Your Actions

- What support and training do families in your school need to build their capacity to support their children academically?

- What can you do at your school to ensure that all families, regardless of language, SES, or prior school experiences, feel empowered to support their children's academic success?

- How can teachers survey students to determine what type of academic support they have at home?

- What professional development do teachers receive regarding family-friendly methods for explaining and providing academic support at home?

- How can communication practices be enhanced so that families can have ongoing dialogues with the teachers and administrators? ●

Strategy 12: Align Family and School Support to Boost Students' Academic Achievement ●

STRATEGIC ALIGNMENT OF ACADEMIC GOALS BETWEEN HOME AND SCHOOL

In an ideal educational world, students have opportunities to explore resources and receive support from their families, the school, and their community. A meta-analysis found that when schools train families on how to assist children with their homework, motivate reading, and use other academically supportive strategies, there is a significant difference in student achievement. The same analysis indicated that the effect is less in secondary grades (Patall et al., 2008). Hence, it is essential to initiate this training for families early in their child's academic journey. In a different study, more evidence was found regarding the positive connection between family engagement in secondary grades and college attendance (Jeynes, 2005).

To promote family empowerment, look for every opportunity to inform families about academic life and opportunities at the school, including providing families with training and two-way discussions regarding academic achievement between teachers and families. Utilize every family gathering to promote these resources and any others that are available strategically. The necessity of involving families in academic conversations and possibilities at school should be a deliberate plan with goals and specifics. It is particularly important for schools serving low SES communities to construct academic involvement and discussion with families. For adequate progress in building academic knowledge, the school needs to meet families where they are and build on their existing academic engagement. Consider discussing special programs and opportunities for academic advances, offering examples of study-friendly atmospheres in the home, promoting reading, and conducting two-way student-centered parent–teacher conferences.

The ultimate goal of family and school partnerships is to strengthen student academic potential and socioemotional balance. Engaging families in high-impact practices alongside school faculty, staff, and administrators values the input of all participants and transforms a consumer–provider relationship into a true partnership. Hattie (2009) asserted that active family partnerships add two or three extra years to a child's education. This has a .51 effect size, well above the .40 hinge point, where results reflect notable differences.

The question is how to effectively form a partnership between schools, families, and the community in a way that supports students academically. According to Angel Harris and Keith Robinson (2016) to truly be a positive force in student achievement, family involvement may need to "maintain a positive trajectory" toward college. They advise that family engagement is not a one-size-fits-all model. In this book, we intend to bring precision to this dilemma by providing specific strategies to create and strengthen school, family, and community partnerships.

Successful implementation of Strategy 12 requires knowing what supports a student can receive at home and how school personnel (teachers and support staff) can fill in the gaps—complement where there is limited academic support or motivate and celebrate where there is steady support. Consider the following case of an educator who understood the urgency of family engagement from her time in the classroom and carried the experience as she moved up the ranks to become a principal.

 ## Aligning the Academic Vision and Action Plan With School and Family

Nestled in a farming community in Arizona, Principal Celia Morgan was recognized for her dedication and attention to detail regarding family and community engagement. Her fourth year as a principal was preceded by 12 years of intense work in this community.

When Celia was a student, her mother had taken great care to ensure that young Celia had a place to study, good lighting, an organized environment, books, and the necessary technology. Her mother also ensured that Celia abided by the calendar and that "study time" was defended from interruptions. As a teacher, she drew on those practices to train her students' families to do the same. Her open school nights, orientation night, and parent–teacher conferences were all opportunities for Ms. Morgan to share her ideas and emphasize the importance of an academic strategy at home.

As a grade leader and department chair, Ms. Morgan made her case to her colleagues that when families are engaged, students behave better, come better prepared to class, and partnerships to support students can be established. As a principal, she trained teachers so that they in turn could train families.

(Continued)

(Continued)

As part of the school's family and community empowerment plan, teachers:

- Conducted surveys on students' studying habits: time, place, etc.
- Conducted surveys on students' access to technology, such as Wi-Fi and computers.
- Created a Family and Community Engagement Committee made up of families and staff.
- Provided teachers with additional monthly planning time to communicate with families.
- Set up a family academy online, with key partners in the community (churches, community centers, etc.) to conduct family training on how to read a report card, the importance of attendance, how to promote good studying habits, tips to encourage reading for fun, and other strategies for academic improvement.

Every person, teacher, or staff member who joined the school understood the urgency of cultivating the family and community engagement that the school wanted to achieve. They all worked together to achieve the school's vision. ●

The power of such a partnership is additive. It must begin at prekindergarten and continue through to 12th grade. The current shift in curriculum and legislative expectations, which moves the beginning of high-stakes schooling from first grade to prekindergarten, has led to an increased achievement gap between low-SES families and minoritized students compared to their middle-class, dominant group peers.

VOLUNTARY PREKINDERGARTEN: KNOWLEDGE IS ACADEMIC POWER

Various states have adopted voluntary prekindergarten (VPK) programs to welcome children before they are of school age. According to the National Center for Education Statistics (NCES; 2021), as of the 2020–21 school year, nearly all states have a VPK program and 41 states have a VPK program guided by comprehensive standards. These programs provide support for student school readiness free of charge. Through their participation in the VPK program, children acquire the "necessary cognitive, social, emotional, and technical skills to comprehend and process" kindergarten instruction (Allee et al., 2022).

However, with the new demands of kindergarten standards, the VPK program is no longer limited to preparing students for the rigors of learning; instead, these programs require students to meet a level of proficiency even before compulsory school attendance begins. Unfortunately, many families in low-SES communities often lack the resources and capacity to fully take advantage of these VPK programs. According to a National Center for Education Statistics report from 2020–21 (NCES, 2021), families' participation in these programs varied according to family income, where wealthier families had a greater percentage of participation than families affected by poverty. Why does this matter? Because nonparticipation exacerbates the achievement gap.

It would be beneficial for schools and districts to conduct a community scan of families with children already enrolled in the school system (who may have younger siblings) as well as families with young children who are not yet enrolled in the district. The community scan could gather valuable information to ascertain why families have not enrolled their young children in the free VPK programs. Unfortunately, some families confuse "voluntary" with "unnecessary." By gathering information on any obstacles that might be preventing families from enrolling, the school can then provide families with the support they need to overcome those obstacles.

To entice families to participate, surveyors can share information regarding the benefits of VPK and the obstacles students will face later on if they don't enroll in VPK. As part of their family and community engagement strategy plan, schools should collaborate with community partners to promote the benefits of VPK programs. Collaborate with your community partners to leverage local resources and support families who face transportation or other challenges that hinder their participation.

ACTION STEPS

 For Putting Your Family and Community Empowerment Team to Work

- Utilize your family and community engagement team to organize a grassroots campaign.
- Educate families in your community regarding the benefits of VPK: children's socialization, developing motor skills, cooperation skills, and acquiring a love of learning.
- Explain how necessary VPK is for future academic success. Let them know that students will fall behind by the time they reach first grade if they do not acquire these academic skills at the same time as their peers.
- Offer support on how to access the free program. Provide information on enrollment dates, the importance of daily attendance, guidance on how to obtain necessary vaccinations, etc.
- Capitalizing on relationships you have built with your community partners, make use of community resources such as buses and vans to spread the word to the larger community.
- Ask community volunteers to drive portable reading libraries stocked with VPK information around the neighborhood.
- Ask community volunteers to organize an enrollment campaign at community centers, local malls, places of worship, and local parks. ●

SELF-EFFICACY AND SUPPORT IN SECONDARY EDUCATION

The opportunity to start school with stronger academic proficiency has a direct impact on academic progress in subsequent years. The body of longitudinal research consistently shows that early literacy skills are critical predictors of long-term academic success. Students who show poor reading proficiency in early grades tend to carry this academic obstacle through high school if left unaddressed. Funchness (2023) simulated a longitudinal study using data from a Central Florida school district and reported that 78% of the students who scored below Level 3 (at grade-level reading) in Grade 1 scored below Level 3 in Grade 3. Furthermore, 83% of students in Grade 10 scored "the same level or one level higher/lower in Grade 10 than they did in Grade 3." Interventions in VPK and early elementary years can significantly alter developmental trajectories, but sustained support is often necessary to maintain gains. These findings underscore the need for early, intensive, and continuous literacy instruction, as well as ongoing partnership with families to support such efforts.

Student self-efficacy and belief are key to the overall success of the learner. Providing acceleration opportunities through advanced placement courses, international baccalaureate courses, dual enrollment courses, and career and technical education courses is one way to provide equitable access to acceleration and support student self-efficacy. However, students represented by low-performing subgroups need the support of an entire community to access this level of education. Mapp and Bergman (2019) outline several strategies for secondary schools to partner with families to improve academic achievement, emotional well-being, and graduation rates. The three-prong approach can be a successful model for secondary education:

- Family Empowerment Teams can work on providing intentional and strategic communication to families regarding what is needed to transition between elementary school, middle school, and high school. Coordinating efforts across these schools in the district to provide families with seamless and consistent information would go a long way to helping families navigate the K–12 experience.

- Family Empowerment Teams can provide workshops and activities to prepare families and students for the transition from high school to college or career. Family Empowerment Teams could offer information sessions on career planning and how to apply to college, career and technical programs, and other postsecondary options.

- Family Empowerment Teams can offer guidance to educate families on how to express their questions or concerns with the school staff. Once the school is aware of students' specific needs, families and the school can work together to create a system of support that disrupts the achievement gap exacerbated by the effects of poverty, special needs, or low English proficiency, and increases the likelihood of success for all.

ACTION STEPS

 For Aligning Family and School Support to Boost Students' Academic Achievement

- Establish ongoing conversations with the families of students in elementary and share the best ways to motivate reading and studying at home.

- Take advantage of major school events to discuss specific academic resources available to the families.

- Share opportunities for advanced classes, extracurricular activities, and other courses or initiatives the school may offer.

- Each teacher should conduct a survey and learn about their students' access to technology or other studying support at home.

- Set up an academic support system for families that are trying to assist their students. There are multiple resources available to families, such as Khan Academy, the U.S. Department of Education, the National Center for Families Learning, and many others.

- Conduct trainings for teachers to coach their families to support their students as they (the families) come to the parent–teacher conference or provide information on where to find their academic support resources online, at the school, or district. ●

Strategy 12: Self-Analysis Questions to Plan Your Actions

1. How does your school systematically collect data on what families need to support students academically at home? Once that data is collected, how does your school address those needs?

2. How is academic data shared with families? What processes are in place to educate families on how to interpret academic data so that families and schools are in alignment?

3. What can school leadership do to support teachers in achieving the goal of aligning support between school and home? What communications should school leadership send out to families and teachers to ensure alignment?

4. How does your school systematically educate families regarding the vision of the school for students' academic success? Are there programs in place to educate families about the importance of early childhood education, reading at home, daily attendance, and career and college planning? ●

CHAPTER TAKEAWAYS

Chapter 6 focuses on empowering families to actively support their children's academic growth through purposeful engagement, goal setting, and systemic school collaboration. Through practical strategies and real-life examples, it illustrates how equipping families, particularly those most marginalized, with knowledge and tools can help bridge achievement gaps, foster social-emotional development, and establish strong school–home partnerships that ultimately lead to improved student outcomes.

- **Empowerment Requires Intentionality:** Family empowerment must be a deliberate school strategy built on mutual trust, cultural responsiveness, and inclusion in decision making.

- **Empowerment Means Partnership:** True family empowerment involves shared goal setting, collaborative work toward mutual goals, clear and

(Continued)

(Continued)

open communication, and training that improves capacity for families and staff.

- **Practical Tools Matter:** Providing families with concrete resources—such as workshops, access to academic portals, and study habit guidance—builds their capacity to support students at home.

- **Early and Ongoing Engagement Is Crucial:** Empowering families from the earliest stages—prekindergarten through secondary—lays a foundation for long-term academic success and equitable outcomes.

REFLECTIVE QUESTIONS

1. In what ways can your school help families overcome barriers such as language, transportation, or unfamiliarity with school systems to become effective academic partners?

2. How can your school ensure that family engagement strategies go beyond surface-level involvement and lead to true empowerment and shared academic responsibility?

3. What systems are in place at your school to regularly train families and staff on supporting academic achievement across diverse student needs?

4. What needs to change to achieve alignment between academic supports at school and at home?

REIMAGINING TRADITIONAL PRACTICES FOR GREATER FAMILY EMPOWERMENT

"No school can work well for children if parents and teachers do not act in partnership on behalf of the children's best interests." ●

—Dorothy H. Cohen (n.d.)

In our fast-paced and demanding society, it is easy to become victims of the hustle and bustle, especially for families. The challenges of everyday life leave little time for meaningful family and school activities. Educators are also juggling multiple demands on their time. As a result, they struggle to find innovative ways to reach out to families and encourage their leadership and participation in school activities. Like safety, academic success, and emotional well-being, participation in school activities is essential to the health and success of school culture. Therefore, in this chapter, we offer busy educators' ideas and practical strategies for how they can collaborate with families to reimagine traditional school practices for family empowerment and improved relationships between home and school.

Additional Tools to Build Family Capacity

THE SCHOOL–FAMILY CALENDAR: A COMMUNICATION TOOL FOR ENGAGEMENT

A school calendar for families may seem passe and rudimentary. However, it serves as a fundamental tool in fostering not only effective communication but also organizational efficiency within your educational institution. Maintaining a family calendar plays a pivotal role in ensuring that all school-related activities and events are meticulously planned, seamlessly executed, and effectively communicated to not only families but also the local community. Here is an in-depth exploration of why establishing and maintaining a shared school calendar is crucial:

1. **Coordination and Alignment:** A school–family calendar acts as a central hub where all relevant information regarding academic and extracurricular activities converges. It allows school administrators, teachers, staff, and even students and families to have a clear and unified view of what is happening throughout the school year. This coordination is crucial to prevent scheduling overlaps and conflicts.

2. **Conflict Prevention:** Scheduling conflicts can disrupt a school's daily operations and cause unnecessary stress for everyone involved. When all key players have access to the same calendar, the chances of double-booking events or inadvertently neglecting important dates are significantly reduced. This, in turn, ensures that activities and events run smoothly and efficiently.

3. **Awareness and Preparation:** A comprehensive school calendar ensures that all members of the school community are well informed about upcoming events and crucial dates. This includes not only academic events, such as examinations, parent–teacher conferences, and

report card distribution, but also nonacademic events, including staff meetings, professional development days, and special school-related activities, such as field trips or fundraisers. Awareness empowers individuals to plan their work and personal commitments accordingly.

4. **Efficient Resource Allocation:** Schools often have limited resources, including staff and facilities. A well-organized calendar allows for the efficient allocation of these resources. For instance, it ensures that staff members are available when needed for events, classrooms are appropriately scheduled, and facilities like gymnasiums or auditoriums are reserved for the right activities.

5. **Improved Family and Student Engagement:** When families and students have access to the school calendar, they can actively participate in school life. They can plan their involvement in activities, attend important meetings, and support school initiatives more effectively. This engagement fosters a stronger sense of community within the school.

6. **Crisis Preparedness:** In the event of unexpected circumstances, such as weather-related closures or emergencies, a well-maintained school calendar can serve as a reference point for rescheduling or adapting plans. It aids in decision making and mitigating the impact of unforeseen disruptions.

7. **Accountability and Evaluation:** A shared school calendar promotes accountability among staff members and administrators. It provides a historical record of events and activities, facilitating retrospective analysis and improvement in future planning.

The creation and maintenance of a school calendar are pivotal to the efficient functioning of your educational institution. Sharing the calendar within the school community fosters coordination, minimizes conflicts, enhances communication, and empowers all involved parties to participate actively in the school's activities and objectives, leading to a harmonious and successful educational environment.

PRIORITIZE FAMILY TIME

School administrators can play a significant role in helping families prioritize family time by promoting a culture that values and discusses family time. Although the focus of this book is singularly honed in on increasing family participation and engagement in school, we are keenly aware that families also need to build their relationships with each other to thrive. Strong families have more capacity to offer their assets to the school community. We list here a few ways that school leadership can support and encourage family time.

1. ***Promote a Balanced Approach to Homework:*** Encourage teachers to assign reasonable amounts of homework and emphasize the importance of quality over quantity. This allows students to complete their assignments efficiently, leaving more time for family activities in the evenings.

2. ***Create Family-Friendly School Policies:*** Implement policies that support family time, such as setting limits on after-school activities and ensuring that school events and meetings are scheduled at convenient times for working families.

3. ***Educate Families on Time Management:*** Offer workshops or resources to families on effective time management and stress the importance of setting aside dedicated family time in their busy schedules.

4. ***Advocate for Limited Screen Time:*** Educate families and students about the adverse effects of excessive screen time on family relationships. This is particularly important, as many school districts are banning smartphones during school hours. This can result in students bingeing on their smartphones when out of school, so it is imperative to encourage families

to establish screen-free times, such as during meals or before bedtime.

5. ***Promote Family Engagement in Education:*** Highlight the benefits of family involvement in a child's education. Encourage families to attend school events and parent–teacher conferences, and participate in school activities that involve the whole family.

6. ***Offer Family-Focused Workshops and Seminars:*** Organize workshops or seminars on topics related to family well-being, parenting skills, and communication within the family unit.

7. ***Provide Resources for Family Activities:*** Share ideas and resources for family-friendly activities, in the school community and through school communication channels. This could include suggestions for local outings, reading lists, or creative projects that families can do together.

8. ***Consider Flexible School Schedules:*** If feasible, consider flexible school schedules that accommodate working families. For instance, offering extended hours for school activities or providing options for before- and after-school care can ease the burden on families.

9. ***Lead by Example:*** School administrators should also lead by example by valuing their own family time and demonstrating a healthy work–life balance. This sets a positive precedent for the entire school community.

10. ***Gather Feedback:*** Regularly seek feedback from families and students about how the school can better support family time. This input can inform future policies and initiatives.

11. ***Host Family-Centric Events:*** Organize events that celebrate families, such as family fun days, picnics, or themed nights at the school. These events can strengthen the sense of community and emphasize the importance of family bonds.

By implementing these strategies and fostering a supportive environment that values family time, school administrators can help families strike a balance between academic commitments and quality time spent together. This not only benefits the well-being of the students but also contributes to a healthier, more engaged school community.

PROMOTE FAMILY VOLUNTEERING

Promoting family volunteering within your school community lays the foundation for a dynamic, collaborative, and engaged learning environment. Family volunteering fosters academic success, strengthens relationships, builds a sense of community, and empowers families to actively engage in their child's education. By embracing diverse roles and creating an inclusive environment, school administrators can inspire and facilitate meaningful family involvement that enriches the educational experience for everyone involved. The following are a few benefits of family volunteering.

1. **Enhanced Academic Success:** Family involvement in school activities has been consistently linked to improved academic outcomes for students. When families volunteer, they gain firsthand insights into their child's learning environment, enabling them to provide better academic support at home. This involvement sends a powerful message to students that their education is a top priority for their family.

2. **Strengthened School–Family Relationships:** Family volunteering establishes and strengthens the vital connection between the school and families. When families actively participate in school life, it creates a more open and collaborative atmosphere. They become partners in their child's education, fostering trust and better communication between educators and families.

3. **A Sense of Community:** Volunteering can foster a profound sense of community within the school. It brings

families together around a shared purpose: supporting their children's growth and development. These connections extend beyond the school gate, contributing to a vibrant and supportive local community.

4. **Development of Diverse Talents:** Encourage families to explore a wide range of volunteer roles that suit their interests, skills, and schedules. Some families may excel at helping in classrooms, whereas others may prefer to assist with school events, fundraising initiatives, beautification projects, extracurricular activities, or organizational leadership. Offering diverse opportunities ensures that all families can find a way to contribute meaningfully.

5. **Modeling for Students:** Family volunteering demonstrates a tangible commitment to the importance of education. When children witness their families actively participating in school activities, it reinforces the value of learning and sets a positive example for lifelong learning.

6. **Building Relationships:** Volunteering at school allows families to form connections with other families, educators, and school staff. These relationships can be a source of valuable support and advice, creating a network that extends beyond school-related activities.

7. **Enhancing the Educational Experience:** Family involvement through volunteering adds depth and richness to the educational experience. Families bring diverse perspectives, talents, and experiences that can enrich classroom discussions and school events. This can lead to more innovative and engaging learning opportunities for students.

8. **Development of Leadership Skills:** Encourage families to take an active role in shaping school policies and decisions through parent–teacher associations or advisory committees. Their input can contribute to school improvement and a more responsive educational environment.

School leadership can further promote and encourage family volunteering by structuring regular recognitions and celebrations of the incredibly valuable work of volunteers. Make a practice of publicly acknowledging the contributions of individual family volunteers during events and in the school newsletter. Honor volunteers with certificates and awards during special school events. Show your appreciation by publicly thanking them for their time and effort to reinforce the value of their involvement and encourage other families to get involved.

To facilitate volunteering, be mindful of families' time constraints and varying schedules. Offer opportunities for in-school and out-of-school involvement, including remote or evening options, to accommodate working families. Strategy 13 offers strategies and opportunities to maximize the impact of parent–teacher conferences.

 **Strategy 13: Maximize Parent–Teacher Conferences** ●

Parent–teacher conferences have long been a foundational component of students' academic and social-emotional well-being. They are a formalized opportunity for families and teachers to come together to celebrate a child's unique talents and achievements, as well as to collaboratively problem solve regarding their challenges and devise strategies for overcoming them. These formal meetings also provide a valuable opportunity to foster positive relationships between families and schools.

As school administrators, your guidance and support in arranging and conducting parent–teacher conferences can significantly impact their outcomes. Consider creative ways you might communicate parent–teacher best practices before they occur. These could be discussed during family meetings or events. Alternatively, perhaps the best practices and tips could be featured as a special section in your newsletter. Here are some of our suggestions for what you might include in your best practices guidance.

1. **Schedule in Advance:** Encourage families to schedule conferences well in advance. Stress that advanced scheduling allows teachers to allocate time for preparation, ensuring that they can provide personalized insights and recommendations for each student. It also helps prevent scheduling conflicts and ensures that all families have an equal opportunity to meet with teachers.

2. **Prepare Ahead of Time:** Emphasize the importance of preparation for families and teachers. Families should take the time to reflect on their child's progress and any specific concerns they wish to address. Teachers should review student records, assessments, and other relevant information to offer informed guidance during the conference.

3. **Communicate and Listen Effectively:** Reinforce the significance of effective communication during conferences. Encourage families to articulate their concerns and questions clearly, while also listening attentively to the teacher's perspective. Foster a respectful and collaborative atmosphere that encourages both parties to actively engage in productive dialogue.

4. **Avoid Assumptions:** Remind families not to make assumptions or jump to conclusions before the conference. Encourage them to approach the meeting with an open mind and a willingness to explore potential solutions and insights offered by teachers.

5. **Be Specific:** Encourage families to be specific about the issues they want to discuss during the conference. The more precise their concerns, the easier it will be for teachers to address them effectively. This specificity ensures that the conference remains focused and productive.

6. ***Facilitate Resolution:*** Emphasize that the goal of parent–teacher conferences is to enhance the student's educational experience. Encourage families and teachers to work together to identify concrete steps and strategies for addressing any challenges or concerns raised during the meeting. Collaborative problem solving is more likely to lead to improved outcomes for students.

7. ***Involve Administrators as Needed:*** Highlight the availability of administrators to mediate or provide additional support during conferences, especially in cases where discussions become contentious or challenging. Administrators can help ensure that the conference remains constructive and solutions oriented.

8. ***Consider Optimal Timing:*** Although there is no ideal time for parent–teacher conferences, provide guidance on optimal scheduling. Suggest that families consider mid-marking period or after the issuance of grades and assessments for more comprehensive discussions about academic progress. We recommend that families consider scheduling conferences at the beginning of the marking period. This timing provides an opportunity to set clear expectations for the upcoming academic term, understand homework policies, and align with the teacher's goals for the class.

9. ***Discuss the Whole Child:*** Encourage teachers and families to consider a wide range of topics for discussion during conferences. In addition to academic matters, these may include strategies for managing homework, extracurricular involvement, social development, and addressing any behavioral concerns. Emphasize that conferences are an opportunity to address the whole student.

10. ***Respect the Teacher's Time:*** Stress the importance of punctuality and attendance. Failing to attend a scheduled conference without prior notice not only disrupts the teacher's schedule but also demonstrates

a lack of respect for their time. Advise families to promptly inform the school office if they need to cancel or reschedule a conference.

11. ***Ask for Teacher Insights:*** Inform families about the valuable insights teachers can provide during conferences. Teachers have a holistic view of students' progress, including factors beyond academics, such as attendance, behavior, attitude, and work habits. Encourage families to leverage this knowledge to support their child's overall development.

When school leadership, teachers, and families all approach parent–teacher conferences thoughtfully and with an optimistic mindset, they are much more likely to be not only beneficial to the student's success but also a more pleasant experience for all involved. By encouraging teachers and families to plan ahead and articulate goals for parent–teacher conferences, these meetings have the potential to be so much more than a hurdle to overcome. They can be opportunities for relationship building and empowerment.

REIMAGINING PARENT–TEACHER CONFERENCES

For families, parent–teacher conferences have long been a cornerstone of the educational experience, offering a vital opportunity to connect with teachers and gain insights into their child's academic journey. However, the traditional format of these conferences can be time consuming, limited in scope, and may not fully capture a student's holistic development. To address these limitations, schools can explore innovative ways to reimagine parent–teacher conferences, fostering deeper engagement and providing a more comprehensive understanding of each student's progress. Here are some transformative approaches:

1. ***Offer Flexible Scheduling:*** Acknowledge that modern families have diverse schedules, and a one-size-fits-all approach may not work. Offer options for families to

schedule conferences during evenings, weekends, or work breaks. Video conferences, though not ideal, might increase participation for families who cannot attend in person.

2. **Provide Continuous Feedback:** Move away from the idea that meaningful communication with teachers only happens during scheduled conferences. Establish communication channels such as email, messaging apps, or online platforms where families can receive regular updates on their child's assignments, test scores, and classroom activities. This ongoing feedback keeps families informed and engaged throughout the school year.

3. **Create Portfolio Presentations:** Instead of relying solely on grades and standardized test scores, develop portfolios that showcase a student's achievements, creativity, and personal growth. These portfolios can include essays, projects, and artwork that provide a comprehensive view of a student's abilities and development over time.

4. **Embrace Goal Setting:** Transform conferences into collaborative goal-setting sessions. Encourage families, students, and teachers to collaborate on setting academic and personal goals. Create action plans that outline specific steps for achieving these goals, fostering a sense of accountability and shared responsibility.

5. **Include Student Reflections:** Promote student self-reflection as a precursor to conferences. Encourage students to write self-assessments, set personal goals, and identify areas where they need support. These reflections provide valuable insights into students' self-awareness and learning experiences.

6. **Draw on Specialized Support Teams:** Utilize multidisciplinary teams within the school to provide

a comprehensive understanding of students' needs. In addition to teachers, involve counselors, special education specialists, and language support staff in conferences to address all aspects of a student's development.

7. **Develop Student Support Plans:** Develop and share personalized student support plans that outline strategies and interventions tailored to students requiring additional assistance. Collaborate with families during conferences to create, implement, and monitor these plans, ensuring a holistic approach to support.

8. **Encourage Teacher Collaboration:** Initiate collaborative conferences involving multiple teachers who work with the same student. This approach enables a comprehensive assessment of the student's strengths and challenges across various subjects and classes, fostering a more holistic perspective.

9. **Involve Community Members:** Enrich conferences by involving community members, mentors, or alumni. These individuals can provide students with real-world insights, career guidance, and inspiration, reinforcing the relevance and purpose of their education.

10. **Make Communication Accessible:** Ensure that language is not a barrier to family–teacher communication. Provide interpretation services or multilingual resources to ensure that all families can participate actively in conferences and effectively engage with teachers.

11. **Seek Feedback:** After each conference, seek feedback from families to refine and improve the conference experience continually. Use surveys to gather insights on format preferences, content relevance, and areas where additional support or information may be needed.

Teaming up at Isabela's Parent–Teacher Conference

On an October morning in Yakima, Washington, Maria Cortez checked her emails before her shift at the orchard. One email in particular caught her attention, "Parent–Teacher Conferences Next Week. Please Schedule in Advance."

Her daughter's K–6 school, committed to cultivating partnerships with families, uses the opportunity of Orientation and Open House nights to assist parents in scheduling conferences with the teachers. As follow-up, families receive a reminder and guidance on what to do. The school's objective is to schedule as many parent–teacher conferences as possible in the first semester, to align with the school's family and community engagement goal.

Maria clicked the link in the email to schedule a meeting with Ms. Jensen, her daughter Isabela's sixth-grade teacher, for the following Wednesday at 4:30 p.m.—just after her shift ended. She also noted the option to meet with the school counselor and the vice principal. She did not schedule those meetings on this particular day, but she appreciated the invitation to do so later.

Over the weekend, Maria sat down with Isabela and reviewed her latest report card and some homework assignments. "Mija (my daughter), is there anything you want me to ask about?" Isabela whispered, "Math is hard. I feel like I am always behind, even when I try." Maria jotted that down and added her own questions: Why was Isabela reluctant to join choir this year? Furthermore, how could she help with homework when she herself never learned Common Core math?

On Wednesday, Maria and Isabela arrived ten minutes before the appointed time. They were greeted courteously by the front office staff. Ms. Cortez was asked if she needed a translator, but she responded that her English was good enough for the conference and that she would rely on Isabela to assist her. At exactly 4:30pm, Ms. Jensen opened the door with a warm smile and invited them in.

"Thank you for coming on time, Ms. Cortez and Isabela," she began. "It is always helpful when families schedule in advance—it gives me time to look closely at each student's progress." Ms. Cortez smiled back, appreciating the fact that Ms. Jensen took the time to review Isabela's school record ahead of time. The room was calm and inviting, with student work displayed on the walls. Ms. Jensen had laid out Isabela's recent math quizzes, reading journal, and behavior log.

"I reviewed Isabela's assessments," the teacher said affirmingly. "She is very thoughtful and articulate in writing, but math is a bit of a challenge right now. She tends to work slowly, which sometimes leads to incomplete assignments." Isabela shyly agreed with this assessment, but her anxiety was quickly alleviated as the teacher affirmed Isabela's hard work and her belief that Isabela was on the path to improvement.

Ms. Cortez leaned forward. "She told me math feels hard. She wants to do well but gets discouraged." "That is helpful to know," Ms. Jensen replied. "Let us think of ways we can support her together." For the next 20 minutes, Ms. Jensen and Ms. Cortez exchanged observations—Ms. Cortez sharing how Isabela sometimes struggled over math work, and Ms. Jensen offered strategies like sending home practice packets and inviting Isabela to join their small tutoring group during lunch. The conversation was positive and reaffirming throughout. Isabela began to feel that, finally, math could be a subject that brought her joy.

After the academic conversation, Ms. Jensen asked what Isabela likes to do at home. Isabela's face lit up, "I like to sing; I love music." Ms. Cortez interjected, "I have been wondering why she did not join the choir." Ms. Jensen paused. "I have noticed she is more reserved this year. It might be a confidence issue—or maybe something else. I will talk to our counselor. If you would like, we could bring her in for a follow-up." Maria nodded. "Yes, por favor."

Ms. Jensen shared how Isabela was a great peer helper in class and had a kind heart. "She is the kind of student who notices when someone is having a rough day," she said. "That is a gift." Isabela's face lit up with pride to hear herself being praised by her mother and teacher.

(Continued)

(Continued)

During the last five minutes of the meeting, they summarized the plan: tutoring twice a week, one follow-up with the counselor, and another check-in in four weeks. Ms. Jensen gave Ms. Cortez her email address and encouraged her to reach out anytime.

Ms. Cortez thanked her for her time and Isabela surprised her with a smile and a hug.

As Ms. Cortez left the school, she noticed the assistant principal nearby. The assistant principal asked how the conference had gone, and both expressed their satisfaction. Ms. Cortez left feeling that the school had thought through these moments, ensuring support was available for every kind of discussion.

That night, Maria and Isabela reflected on the conversation, "She said you are kind and helpful—and that is just as important as good grades."

Isabela grinned and hugged her mamá. "Maybe I will try choir again next semester." ●

This vignette illustrates how a school can set the tone for success. The teachers had been trained on maximizing the outcome of parent–teacher conferences, and they understood and stepped up to this commitment. Most importantly, the family was invited to be an active participant in the design of the plan and its implementation. This resulted in a collaborative effort to provide support for Isabela. How have you found ways to innovate and infuse depth and connection in your family–teacher conferences?

One practice we find to be very promising in reimagining parent–teacher conferences is to offer enough support, guidance, modelling, and practice so that students themselves can lead the meeting. This requires students to take ownership of their own learning and plans for improvement. Student-led conferences have the potential to empower students as well as their families as they find ways to work together toward meeting the student's goals.

ACTION STEPS

For Innovating with Student-Led Conferences

A student-led conference is a preplanned meeting in which students demonstrate responsibility for their academic performance by reviewing their work for families and teachers. Students lead by presenting work samples and discussing their learning, strengths, weaknesses, and progress toward their goals.

- Students prepare and organize work samples, demonstrate learning, and plan next steps.
- Students lead the conversations. They showcase their learning and, in turn, receive feedback from their families and teachers.
- Students take more ownership of their learning.
- Families and students have open communication about school, after-school activities, and other important decisions. ●

Strategy 13: Self-Analysis Questions to Plan Your Actions

1. What pain points are you currently experiencing with your parent–teacher conferences? Which (if any) of the best practices here would help address those trouble spots?

2. What is working really well with your parent–teacher conferences? How can you scale that success to ensure that all teachers and families have a positive experience with conferences?

3. Which of these innovations do you think would be most challenging to implement in your school? Why? What structural changes could you make to facilitate the implementation of that innovation? ●

In the next session, we present the final strategy, Strategy 14 Transform Open House into a Relationship-Building Event. For school to continue improving toward more inclusive and inter-active environment for families and communities, they must consider enriching their current practices. This improvement requires paradigm shifts that transform traditional practices.

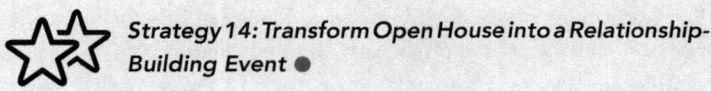

Strategy 14: Transform Open House into a Relationship-Building Event ●

Orientation and Open House events are vital components of a thriving school community. Administrators who meticulously plan and execute these events create a foundation for last-ing engagement, transparent communication, and a sense of unity among families, ultimately enhancing the educational experience for all. Organized with vision, these events can help bridge the gap between schools and families, ensuring that the entire school ecosystem operates harmoniously. Here are just a few ways these events facilitate engagement and connection:

1. **Welcoming New Families:** For families new to the school community, the first impression is crucial. Orientation and Open House nights provide a warm welcome, helping new families transition smoothly into the school environment. A positive experience sets the tone for a productive partnership between the school and families.

2. **Providing Information:** These events should be well-organized opportunities for knowledge sharing. Families receive valuable insights into the school's programs, procedures, and overall culture, which empowers them to participate actively in their child's educational journey.

3. **Updating Returning Families on Recent Changes:** Returning families often appreciate updates on changes and improvements within the school. This is

an opportunity for administrators to communicate any changes in curricula, policies, or facilities, ensuring that all families are kept informed.

4. **Introducing Teachers and Staff:** Personal connections are fundamental to effective communication and problem solving. Meeting teachers and staff members in a friendly and relaxed setting fosters trust and encourages families and students to reach out when they have questions or concerns.

5. **Explaining the Curriculum:** Providing insights into the curriculum demystifies the learning process. Families gain a better understanding of what their children will be studying, which facilitates meaningful conversations at home and supports their children's educational progress.

6. **Reestablishing Homework Goals:** Clear communication about homework policies helps families strike the right balance between academics and extracurricular activities. It emphasizes the importance of a well-rounded education and sets expectations for both students and families.

7. **Promoting Diverse Communication Channels:** It is vital to stress the importance of effective communication channels. By showcasing various methods, such as email, parent–teacher conferences, and online platforms, families are empowered to stay engaged and informed throughout the school year.

8. **Showcasing Classrooms:** Allowing families to visit classrooms is a window into their child's daily educational experiences. It demystifies the learning process and fosters a deeper connection between the home and school environments.

9. **Highlighting Extracurriculars:** Extracurricular activities are not mere add-ons; they are integral to holistic education. By highlighting their value, families

are encouraged to support their child's participation, which can lead to personal growth and the acquisition of new skills.

10. **Celebrating School Spirit:** Igniting school spirit and pride is essential for building a strong school community. These events are perfect opportunities to celebrate student achievements, share success stories, and promote a sense of belonging among families.

11. **Providing Resources:** Offering resources and materials to take home demonstrates the school's commitment to ongoing support. Pamphlets, handbooks, and contact information for school personnel serve as references for families throughout the year.

12. **Encouraging Engagement:** These events should serve as catalysts for ongoing family engagement and empowerment. Encourage families to take an active role in school life throughout the academic year.

In the same way that parent–teacher conferences can be reimagined as student-led conferences, Open House might be reimagined as an interactive experience rather than a one-way communication from teachers to families. There are many ways schools might structure an interactive Open House experience. Here we present one option from Noguera Middle School.

 ## An Interactive Open House Experience

At Noguera Middle School in New Rochelle, New York, Open House had always followed a predictable routine: teachers gave presentations, families took notes, and students sat quietly. Principal Olson wanted to reimagine Open House to ensure that families would become actively engaged and empowered rather than attend as passive recipients of a one-way conversation.

In the new version of Open House, students proudly guided their families through different engagement areas and interactive stations, and staff welcomed them like honored guests.

Station 1: Math in Action

Families sat with their children to solve a real-world math problem. The teacher guided families in a fun, interactive way, demonstrating how families could support learning at home while giving them a chance to practice the new skill during the event.

Station 2: Meet the Teachers

Instead of standing in front of the class, teachers hosted small-group conversations at round tables, answering questions and getting to know each family personally.

Station 3: Tech Hub

Families visited a tech table where staff assisted them in logging into the parent portal, signing up for school text alerts, and accessing online learning tools.

Station 4: Community Connection

A group of local organizations, multilingual family leaders, and school counselors shared resources on mental health, tutoring, and financial assistance.

Student Showcase: Learning in Action

Students proudly shared their latest projects, explaining their learning in their own words—an empowering moment for students and families.

As the event wrapped up, Principal Olson saw something she had never seen before:

- Families lingering, engaged in deep conversations with teachers.
- Families exchanging contact information to stay connected.
- Students leading their families with excitement, not just observing.

For the first time, Open House was more than a meeting—it was a celebration of partnership. Families left feeling valued, informed, and ready to support their children's education. ●

ACTION STEPS

 For Reimagining Open House as an Interactive Experience

• **Build Interactive Engagement Stations.** Create stations where families participate in activities related to their child's learning. Use a rotational model where families move through different engagement areas.

• **Provide Personalized Family Connections.** Families interact with teachers in small-group discussions or one-on-one conversations, rather than passively listening to a whole-group lecture.

• **Cultural and Community Inclusion.** In a welcoming and sensitive manner, integrate the school culture of inclusion and cultural acceptance with the cultural attributes families and communities organically bring to the school.

• **Facilitate Student-Centered Showcases.** Students demonstrate their learning (explaining the physics involved during a model volcano explosion, offering a minimath lesson, reading an original poem, sharing an uncommonly known aspect of history, explaining an art technique, etc.).

• **Lead Math & Literacy Games.** Families engage in hands-on activities that model how to support learning at home.

• **Provide Accessibility.** Provide childcare, translators, and flexible scheduling to remove barriers to attendance.

• **Be Culturally Inclusive.** Include welcome signs in the home languages of students, ask families to contribute to food stations that share their ethnic cuisines, and during transition times, play music from students' various cultures. ●

Transforming long held and established practices into new and unfamiliar formats is a challenging task. It requires planning, collaboration, and buy-in from a diversity of parties involved. It also requires systemic support. To successfully implement a plan of action that leads to change, ensure you gather feedback and input from key players. You might not achieve complete success in the first year. However, ideally, continual revision and sincere attention to feedback should lead to improvement over time.

Strategy 14: Self-Analysis Questions to Plan Your Actions

1. Why is shifting from passive presentations to active participation important?

2. What can you do at your school to ensure that Open House is inclusive and culturally responsive?

3. What ways can you think of to get families and students more involved and empowered in the planning and delivery of the Open House experience for your school? ●

CHAPTER TAKEAWAYS

This chapter invites educators to reimagine events as opportunities for engagement, transforming them from passive, school-led presentations into participatory, student-centered experiences that foster relationships and trust.

- Use a School Calendar to Promote Inclusion: A shared calendar helps align community members, prevent scheduling conflicts, and ensure that all families are informed and prepared to engage meaningfully in school life.

- Promote and Support Family Time: Schools can help families balance academic and personal life by offering flexible scheduling, homework policies that prioritize family time, and family-friendly school practices.

- Expand Volunteering Beyond Traditional Roles: Offering diverse, accessible volunteer opportunities, including virtual and non-school-hour roles, enables more families to contribute their time and talents, enriching school culture and student success.

(Continued)

(Continued)

- Reimagining parent–teacher conferences can lead to more authentic relationship building and make families feel more empowered as advocates for their child's academic success.

- Reimagining Open House can lead to more enjoyable and meaningful experiences where families have the opportunity to interact with their teachers, their children, and engage with the curriculum in dynamic ways.

REFLECTIVE QUESTIONS

1. Looking at your parent–teacher conferences at your school: How can the process be maximized? Does the school conduct training to build teacher capacity in opening lines of communication and support for students?

2. How can you sustain authentic family engagement throughout the school year, not just during Open House or conferences?

3. Consider reimagining parent–teacher conferences at your school. What are five elements you are looking to include?

CONCLUSION

Embracing Family Empowerment

In this book we have presented the 14 strategies that we have seen breathe life into authentic family and community engagement. From vision to implementation, from asset-based mindsets to transformative leadership, each chapter has offered not only a framework but also a call to action: to recognize families not as bystanders or clients, but as coeducators, leaders, and equal partners in the shared responsibility of educating our children.

We began by grounding our work in vision—a critical step in any meaningful change. Schools and districts that craft context-specific engagement plans tailored to their unique populations send a clear message: "We see you. We value you. We are planning with you in mind." When schools take the time to align their goals with the lived realities of families, engagement shifts from an obligation to an opportunity. The vignettes of parents whose needs were initially misunderstood—and later acknowledged and embraced—remind us that deficit-based perceptions must be checked and relationships built with cultural humility and authentic inquiry.

As we moved into collaborative goal setting and decision making, we asked: Who holds the power in schools? Whose voices shape improvement plans? The power of consistent communication and shared goals—seen in the stories of families newly empowered to speak to their school's direction—underscored that inclusion must go beyond invitations to events. Authentic engagement means positioning families as architects of the school's future, not just recipients of the work of others.

To engage families effectively, we must address the barriers that silence them. Too often, educators operate under deficit-based assumptions, believing that some families are "uninvolved" or "unconcerned." However, as the chapters on mindset shift revealed, families engage in ways rooted in culture, experience, and trust. When schools actively name and dismantle deficit thinking, they begin to create the psychological safety necessary for equitable partnerships.

Our most profound transformation comes when families are invited not only to participate, but also to lead. In sharing stories like that of Ms. Feliz in Chapter 2 who transformed her frustration into advocacy, or Doña Jilma Cabral in Chapter 3 who used her community knowledge to support families and students at school, we witnessed the power of centering the knowledge families bring. When storytelling, cultural traditions, and lived experience are welcomed into the curriculum, students see their communities honored and thrive academically and emotionally as a result.

Trust is the heartbeat of every relationship. Without it, no strategy, plan, or initiative can truly succeed. We learned that trust is cultivated in moments of respect, curiosity, and transparency. From Doña Jilma to Principal Calles, we saw that trust is built when educators greet, listen, and learn. It is fortified when safety, physical and psychological, is prioritized. Furthermore, it becomes a school-wide asset when the environment signals care, consistency, and cultural understanding.

Building capacity is not just for staff; it is also for families. Families want to support their children's academic success, but they need schools to meet them halfway. We explored strategies that align home and school learning, ensuring academic goals are not lost in translation between teacher conferences and kitchen tables. The stories of families who learned to navigate educational systems—and eventually shaped them—remind us that capacity leads to agency, and agency leads to change.

This book also elevated the critical role of community partnerships. Schools cannot do this work alone. Whether partnering with local businesses, health providers, cultural organizations, or community leaders, schools expand their reach and relevance when they serve as hubs of community pride and resilience. The pandemic taught us that schools are more than academic institutions—they are trusted messengers, meal providers, safe havens, and emotional anchors. Strengthening these roles through intentional partnerships only deepens the trust families place in schools.

Finally, we reimagined traditional school practices such as Open Houses and conferences, by flipping the script to prioritize relationships over routines. These strategies emphasize that families should not just attend events—they should shape them. Every space where families are present should be a space where they feel a sense of ownership, dignity, and belonging.

A Call to Collective Action

What lies ahead is not easy, but it is essential. It requires disrupting comfort, redistributing power, and redefining what success means. It calls us to move beyond compliance and toward courageous conversations, ongoing reflection, and systems rooted in equity. This is a journey not of isolation, but of collective possibility.

To all educators, leaders, and family members reading this: the work of family and community empowerment is the work of justice. It is the work of rewriting the narrative for students who have been overlooked, families who have been underestimated, and communities that have been marginalized. It is how we build schools that are not just places of learning, but engines of hope.

We invite you now—not just to reflect, but to act. Revisit your plans. Engage in your own self-analysis. Reimagine your calendars, your language, your professional learning, and your partnerships. Reinvest in the belief that families are not problems to solve, but partners to empower. The pages of this book will end, but the story continues—in your classrooms, in your offices, in your living rooms, in every space where school and community intersect. And in those intersections lies the future of education—a future that is more inclusive, more relational, and more powerful because it is built together.

REFERENCES

Allee, K.A., Clark, M.H., Bai, H., & Roberts, S.K. (2022). Direct and indirect impacts of voluntary pre-kindergarten on kindergarten readiness and achievement. *Early Childhood Education Journal, 52*(2), 319–331. https://doi.org/10.1007/s10643–022–01436-w

Angell, S.R., Bass, H.P., Meisinger, R.E., Marcus, M.J., & Sheridan, S.M. (2016). *Achieving academic success for your student through family school partnerships: A TAPP research brief.* Nebraska Center for Research on Children, Youth, Families, and Schools.

Castillo Kickbusch, C. (2023). *FLI practitioner training conference.* https://www.easleadership.com/

Cohen, D.H. (n.d.). https://www.azquotes.com/quote/1142196?utm_source=chatgpt.com#google_vignette

Coleman, M. (2013). *Empowering family-teacher partnerships: Building connections within diverse communities.* SAGE.

Collado, W. (2008). *Parents, don't forget your homework.* Plantation, FL: Vamco Education.

Collado, W. (2025). *Four pillars to guide visionary educators: Structuring schools that serve students in poverty.* Corwin.

Covey, S. (1989). *The 7 habits of highly effective people.* New York: Free Press.

Department of Education, National Center for Education Statistics. (2021). *The condition of education 2021* (NCES 2021–144). https://nces.ed.gov/pubs2021/2021144.pdf

Dowd, A.J., Friedlander, E., Jonason, C., Leer, J., Sorensen, L., Guajado, J., & Pisani, L. (2017). Lifewide learning for early reading development. *New Direction for Children and Adolescent Development, 155,* 31–49.

Dugan, J. (2022). *Co-constructing family engagement 80*(1). https://www.ascd.org/el/articles/co-constructing-family-engagement

Epstein, J.L., & Sheldon, S.B. (2023). *School, family, and community partnerships: Preparing educators and improving schools* (3rd ed.). Routledge, Taylor & Francis Group. https://doi.org/10.4324/9780429400780

Flamboyan Foundation. (2023). *Academic partnering toolkit for administration.* https://flamboyanfoundation.org/

Funchness, A. (2023). *School District of Osceola County literacy longitudinal analysis* [Unpublished manuscript]. Osceola, FL: School District of Osceola County.

Garbacz, S.A., Zerr, A.A., Dishion, T.J., Seeley, J.R., & Stormshak, E. (2018). Parent educational involvement in middle school: Longitudinal influences on student outcomes. *The Journal of Early Adolescence, 38*(5), Article 5. https://doi.org/10.1177/0272431616687670

Gerzon-Kessler, A. (2019). Involving families: A relationship-centered approach. *Educational Leadership, 77*(4). https://www.ascd.org/el/articles/involving-families-a-relationship-centered-approach

Hair, N.L., Hanson, J.L., Wolfe, B.L., & Pollak, S.D. (2015). Association of child poverty, brain development, and academic achievement. *JAMA Pediatrics, 169*(9), 822. https://doi.org/10.1001/jamapediatrics.2015.1475

Harris, A.L., & Robinson, K. (2016). A new framework for understanding parental involvement: Setting the stage for academic success. *RSF: The Russell Sage Foundation Journal of the Social Sciences, 2*(5), 186–201. https://doi.org/10.7758/RSF.2016.2.5.09

Hattie, J. (2009). *Visible learning: A synthesis of over 800 meta-analyses relating to achievement* (Reprinted). Routledge.

Hoglund, W.L.G., Jones, S.M., Brown, J.L., & Aber, J.L. (2015). The evocative influence of child academic and social-emotional adjustment on parent involvement in inner-city schools. *Journal of Educational Psychology, 107*(2), Article 2. https://doi.org/10.1037/a0037266

Hsiao, Y., Higgins, K., & Diamond, L. (2018). Parent empowerment: Respecting their voices, *Teaching Exceptional Children* (No. 1), *51*(1), Article 1.

Jeynes, W.H. (2005). A meta-analysis of the relation of parental involvement to urban elementary school student academic achievement. *Urban Education, 40*(3), 237–269. https://doi .org/10.1177/0042085905274540

Mapp, K., & Bergman., E. (2019). *Dual capacity-building framework for family-school partnership* (Version 2). Retrieved from www.dualcapacity.org

Mapp, K.L., & Bergman, E. (2021). *Embracing a new normal: Toward a more liberatory approach to family engagement.* Carnegie Corporation.

Michigan Department of Education. (2011). *Strategies for strong parent and family engagement.* https://resources .finalsite.net/images/v1692196253/nwschoolsorg/ crzzlixwgdtn6qczd7kw/4a__final_toolkit_without_ bookmarks_370151_7.pdf

Milner, H.R. (2020). *Start where you are, but don't stay there: Understanding diversity, opportunity gaps, and teaching in today's classrooms* (Second ed.). Harvard Education Press.

National Association for Family, School, and Community Engagement. (2023). *Family engagement core competencies: A body of knowledge, skills, and dispositions for family-facing professionals.* https://nafsce.org/page/CoreCompetencies

Noguera, P., Hurtado, A., & Fergus, E. (Eds.). (2012). *Invisible no more: Understanding the disenfranchisement of Latino men and boys.* Routledge.

Patall, E., Cooper, H., & Robinson, C. (2008). Parent involvement in homework: A research synthesis, *Review of Educational Research 78*(4), 1039–1101.

Payne, R. K. (2005). *A framework for understanding poverty* (4th ed). Highlands, TX: aha! Process.

Spangler, D. (n.d.). https://quotefancy.com/quote/1588512/ David-Spangler-Some-people-think-they-are-in-community- but-they-are-only-in-proximity

Watson, S., Vernon, L., Seddon, S., Andrews, Y., & Wang, A. (2016). Parents influencing secondary students' university aspirations: A multilevel approach using school-SES. *Issues in Educational Research, 26*, 673–693. http://www.iier.org .au/iier26/watson.pdf

INDEX

Free professional learning from leading education experts

 **Live and on-demand webinars**

Get a certificate for PD hours!

 **Videos**

 **Podcasts**

 **Study guides**

 **New teacher toolkit**

 **Lessons and strategies**

 **Checklists and assessments**

 **Plain language summaries of education research**

 **Book excerpts**

 **Other downloadables**

 **Blogs**

Leave a review!
If you enjoyed this book, let us know by leaving a review on **GoodReads.com** or **Amazon.com**.

corwin.com/resources

CORWiN

CORWIN

To help every educator help every student

We believe that every single student deserves a great education

We believe that knowing our impact is both a privilege and a responsibility

We believe that a fair, stable, and thriving society is built on education